WARRIORS FOR THE FAITH

FIRST-PERSON STORIES FROM THE BIBLE

TIM RUPP

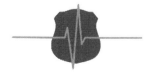

Warriors for the Faith

First-Person Stories from the Bible

by Tim Rupp

ISBN: 978-0-692-06294-4

Author Contact Info: office@thestrongblueline.org

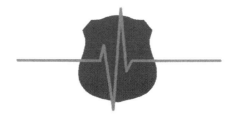

The Strong Blue Line
Idaho Falls, ID
TheStrongBlueLine.org

CONTENTS

ACKNOWLEDGMENTS

Special thanks to Mrs. Trisha Randall for her editing.

To warriors of the faith who faithfully engage the enemy.

"Be sober-minded; be watchful. Your adversary the devil prowls around like a roaring lion, seeking someone to devour. Resist him, firm in your faith, knowing that the same kinds of suffering are being experienced by your brotherhood throughout the world."
(1 Peter 5:8-9)

PREFACE

Life is a story.

Today's most popular forms of entertainment are movies and novels —they tell stories. Stories of love, friendship, betrayal, competition, murder, and war. A good movie or book places us "in" the action. We feel like we can relate to, and understand the characters. We cheer for the hero and disdain the villain. Two-thirds of the Bible is written in historical narrative—stories about people. Jesus taught using stories. The stories in the Bible are replete with drama, mystery, and even humor. Like popular movies and novels, Bible stories have intriguing plots of love, friendship, betrayal, competition, murder, and war. Why then do they seem so boring? Why do we have trouble relating to the characters?

There are two reasons. First, we miss the drama because we are not familiar with the culture and setting of the stories. Second, we approach biblical stories like half the people walked around wearing halos and the other half wore horns, and everyone talked in old English.

In this book I take biblical narratives and put "flesh" on the characters. The stories are about famous warriors, kings, and prophets of old. But, they are also stories about every day, common people, like you and me. While common people are not considered warriors, many are. In fact, most warriors are just common folks—people who are willing to face and engage the enemy. Former army ranger and West Point professor, Lt. Col. Dave Grossman say warriors are those who have the authority and capability to march toward the sound of the gun (face interpersonal human aggression) and return fire (operate under those conditions). Lt. Col. Grossman speaks this of warriors for their country, but there are also warriors for their faith.

Warriors for the Faith are not always called to march toward literal gunfire, but they are called to face the enemy. The enemies of faith warriors face are just as real and dangerous as any physical enemy. Believers are called to "stand against the schemes of the devil" and "against the authorities, against the cosmic powers over this present darkness, against the spiritual forces of evil" (Ephesians 6:11-12). Not only are Warriors for the Faith called to stand against forces of evil but to engage them, "For we do not wrestle against flesh and blood, but against the rulers, against the authorities, against the cosmic powers over this present darkness" (6:12a).

In this book, through artistic liberty, I tell Bible stories from the lips of those who lived them. While I take the liberty to create much of the backstories, I have researched the historical and cultural settings and exegeted the biblical text in an effort to remain accurate to the biblical truths and principles presented in the Bible, while at the same time telling a memorable and realistic story. My goal is to take readers back in time, and place them in the middle of the action. By doing so I hope the stories will come alive, the biblical truths will be revealed, and the principles applied in your own life.

Life is a story.

Everyone has a story. What's your story?

Tim Rupp
January 2018

1

A WARRIOR WITH A PROBLEM

My name is Naaman, and I'd like to tell you a story, my story to be more precise. You might call it a "testimony" because it's the story of how God worked in my life—and changed me forever.

I was a soldier who served in the army my whole adult life. Countless men's lives were shed on my blade. I was good at my job and quickly rose through the ranks to become a general. Now, general is the highest rank in the military and there may be many generals, but there's only one top general. In the United States that title is General of the Armies. America has only two generals who held this rank: General George Washington; and the World War I General John Pershing. That's what I became, the General of the Armies, the one top general.

My story takes place long before Pershing or even Washington. It was in the ninth century BC when I ranked as the supreme commander of the Syrian army. Syria is located in what today is known as the Middle East. Syria is north of that pesky little nation known as Israel. Israel, as a nation, hadn't been around all that long. Her first king was a man named Saul

—that was around 1050 BC, and about 200 years before my time. After Saul and his son Jonathan were killed in battle, a prominent warrior named David became king. David's son Solomon and then his grandson Rehoboam reigned. But Rehoboam, being a foolish spoiled brat, tried to push his weight around and in 931 BC, the kingdom split. Rehoboam was left with the southern part of the kingdom, which became known as Judah while a guy named Jeroboam became king in the north retaining the name Israel—this was the Israel I was familiar with.

For my entire life, Israel was a pain to deal with. It's a little, no-count country whose kings, politics, and religious loyalties changed more often than the weather. In a short 57 years, Israel was on their eighth king—a man named Ahab. Ahab's son Joram was Israel's king when I served as supreme commander of the Syrian army.

As I said when I began, I want to tell you my story. The story of how my life was drastically changed. I was a proud man, but I was a hurting man. I carried a burden that even I couldn't shake. I sought relief everywhere. People suggested this remedy or that one; they recommended I speak to this specialist or that one. They told me pray to this god, or that god. And I did everything they said, but I still carried this burden with me every day. I'd almost given up hope, but I didn't. Or rather, my wife didn't give up hope. She was certain there was some way I could beat this thing. She had faith that there was something—or someone—more powerful than my burden.

However, in the beginning even her faith didn't bring me relief. My pain and desperation caused me to be short-tempered often flying into a rage. I had no use for slackers, complainers, and for those who weren't willing to push themselves. My pride told me that if I could push myself through my pain, then others should push themselves, too. Yes, I was an angry man. But then an amazing event took place in my life. Relief came from the most unexpected place and I was changed. Oh, boy was I ever changed!

Some of you may doubt my story, but the Bible records it. I invite you to read along while I share. It is found in Second Kings, chapter five. I served under King Ben-Hadad, king of Syria, who reigned from 900-860 BC.[1] Remember, I was a proud man. Proud of who I was and my accomplishments? You bet I was. The entire Syrian army was under my command. Position? I had it. Power? I had it. Prestige? I had it.

The biblical record shows how respected I was. *Naaman, commander of the army of the king of Syria, was a great man with his master and in high favor.* Hear that? *...a great man with his master and in high favor.* Why did King Ben-Hadad like me so much? Because I made him look good! I was a successful military commander and it was *by me* Syria was feared among the nations, the biblical text continues, *...because by him* [that's me] *the Lord had given victory to Syria.*

Oh, but it doesn't stop there, continue on! Look what else is said of me, *He was a mighty man of valor.* Some of your other English translations say, *a mighty warrior,* or *a valiant soldier.* In the original language, the word translated *valor* means strength, might, efficiency, ability, or force.[2] Yeah, that pretty much sums up who I was. You Americans would say I was a self-made man, a man's man, the kind of man your famous singer sung about in the song, *I did it my way.*

I accomplished great things in my life. No one ever gave me anything... or so I thought. My pride told me I made my king look good because of my strength and valor, but I want to point out something in the text that the biblical writer included. *Naaman, commander of the army of the king of Syria, was a great man with his master and in high favor, because by him the Lord had given victory to Syria.* Did you see that little phrase, *the Lord had given victory*? I understand it now, but I didn't at the time.

You see, I believed gods were territorial and that there were many of them. They ruled over their nations with varying degrees of strength and proved it in battle with a winner and a loser. Everyone thought Israel's God was once strong, because we all knew the stories of how Israel came up from Egyptian slavery and practically walked into the land conquering city after city in what they called the Promised Land. But during my lifetime, Israel was anything but a worthy adversary and nothing could have prepared me to recognize Israel's God as the one, supreme God of all. However, I soon learned that, indeed, the God of Israel was truly the one giving me victory even as an unbeliever. Of course, it wasn't for my purposes, but his. At the time, I thought everything was about me; imagine that!

Yes, I was a proud man. I was a valiant soldier, a commander second to none, I led my country to victory, and I was honored by my king. I had it all. But, there was something else I had. I had a burden I couldn't shake.

A single word towards the end of verse one speaks volumes: *but*. Do you know what that means? In English, that little conjunction *but* is a game changer. All the accolades about me being a great soldier, having great position, power, and prestige are all tainted because—*but*—*but he was a leper* Yep, for all my accomplishments I was ultimately a leper. I had this stinking, infectious disease that slowly disfigures and maims its victims before finally killing them. It causes severe sores to erupt across the surface of the skin and destroys nerves so that fingers and toes simply drop off. Leprosy was fatal when I had it, so you can imagine how motivated I was to get rid of it![3] I'd have given up everything just to be cured from that awful disease. Position, you could have it. Power, take it. Prestige, it matters not—I was a leper.

Naaman, commander of the army of the king of Syria, was a great man with his master and in high favor, because by him the Lord had given victory to Syria. He was a mighty man of valor, but he was a leper. (2 Kgs. 5:1)

At first I denied it. Not me, the great Naaman! The doctors were simply wrong. Surely, they mistook the early symptoms for something else. But eventually, I had to face the facts. I became angry, and the "Not me!" turned to "Why me?" I fought the fiercest of warriors in battle, men bigger than I, armies that outnumbered me. I always came out on top. I beat them. I won. No one could defeat the valiant Naaman. But this burden was a foe unlike any other, and I could not win.

Still, I traveled far and wide seeking relief. I spent untold sums of money on all kinds of quacks claiming they had a cure. "Put this ointment on," "Try this medication," "Eat this herb," "Drink this potion," but no relief. I wasn't much of a religious person, but I even tried that religious stuff too. I prayed to Rimmon, the Syrian god my king worshiped—nothing. I brought money and all the sacrifices the priests required—nothing. Every time we defeated another nation I inquired of their gods—nothing. And heaven knows how my wife prayed for relief. I would find her bowed down before her idols praying to her gods—still nothing. I was ready to give up. But, I was never known for weakness, and I was determined that this would be no different. I would figure out how to deal with it—my way.

Speaking of my wife, what a treasure she was. Between you and me, I don't know how she put up with me. Proud, arrogant, and egotistical is how I'd describe myself. Not to mention short-tempered and angry all the time. Then to top it all off she had to watch her husband physically deteriorate before her eyes. I didn't appreciate her like she deserved unless I was off to war. Several months hanging around a bunch of smelly, sweaty, loud, and foulmouthed soldiers really made me miss my dear wife. I always brought her back some trinket, earrings, a necklace, or perhaps some fine silk.

But the best present, by far, that I ever brought home was from one of those raids against, you guessed it, that pesky little nation of Israel. I brought home a little girl from Israel to help her around the house. What a surprise that was! It was better than one of those new-fangled automatic dishwashers Americans brag about! Mrs. Naaman didn't even have to pick-up and rinse the dishes!

Now the Syrians on one of their raids had carried off a little girl from the land of Israel, and she worked in the service of Naaman's wife. (2 Kgs. 5:2)

Surprisingly, this little girl got along very well with my wife. Those Israelites were good for something—they made great slaves! From the beginning, my wife told me how sweet the girl was and how willingly she did her work. I didn't understand it. I'd catch them laughing and carrying on, baking or sewing together— more like a mother and a daughter than a master and a slave. Oh well, I figured this was better than my wife's cats. At least the girl could pull her own weight.

She said to her mistress, "Would that my lord were with the prophet who is in Samaria! He would cure him of his leprosy." (2 Kgs. 5:3)

Little did I know; that this young Israelite slave girl would be the catalyst for the biggest change in my life. One day when my wife and her new slave—or should I say, her new "daughter"— were cleaning up the house, she said something to my wife. I didn't hear it, but the Bible records she said, "Would that my lord were with the prophet who is in Samaria! He would cure him of his leprosy."

I got home late from work that evening and expected to find my wife sound asleep. I quietly made my way into our bedroom and was surprised to find her waiting up and eager to share with me the good news. "There's a man in Samaria that can cure you!" she said excitedly. But her joy soon turned into sadness when she heard my angry response. To tell you the truth, I was so angry I could put my fist through the wall. Here we go again with another magical cure-all. Another quack that just wants money. Another hopeless dream of relief. Another religious nut. Why? Why go through this again? Why put myself through it? Why put my wife through it? My anger grew into a rage, and I lashed out verbally. I'm sure I woke everyone in the house.

My sweet wife didn't say anything. It used to be that she'd give it right back, but not this time. She just told me I should think about it and that she'd pray for me. We turned in for the night, but I didn't get much sleep. My wife had changed since this girl from Israel came to live with us. She seemed happier, more content. I also noticed she stopped praying to her gods. In fact, the furniture was rearranged—not that that was unusual, but the idols were gone. To whom was she praying? After tossing and turning, thinking about these questions, I finally drifted off to sleep.

By the time I awoke the next morning, my wife was already up and making breakfast—no sign of the girl, who normally prepared our meals. No mention of what was spoken the night before either—just small talk. I gave her a kiss and she gently squeezed my hand. She knew I was experiencing more and more pain from the leprosy. I turned and headed out the door. As I walked across the courtyard, I glanced back to see her standing on the patio watching me walk away. "Okay, okay. I'll talk to the king and see if he'll let me go to Samaria to see this 'prophet man.'" She smiled. I simply turned away and trudged forward.

It'd be all for naught anyway. Although the king liked and respected me, he was a stern administrator and a responsible leader of Syria. I honestly didn't think he'd agree to let the commander of his army run off on some wild goose chase, but I told my wife I'd ask. I arrived at work and checked my schedule. A mid-morning meeting with the king was already on my agenda. "I'll just mention it, get turned down, and then get on with business," I thought. Our meeting was set for ten, so at 9:50 I reported to the king's aides and was surprised to be ushered in immediately. I will admit, I was taken aback by their promptness; I'm usually waiting thirty minutes past our appointment time to see the king. When I entered, I figured that I might as well get it over with quickly and make it clear that it wasn't my idea. "Thus and so spoke the girl from the land of Israel," I said, explaining about the prophet in Samaria.

So Naaman went in and told his lord, "Thus and so spoke the girl from the land of Israel." And the king of Syria said, "Go now and I will send a letter to the king of Israel." So he went, taking with him ten talents of silver, six thousand shekels of gold, and ten changes of clothing. (2 Kgs. 5:4-5)

If you think I was astonished by my timely appointment, you should have seen me thrown for a loop at the king's response, "Go now and I will send a letter to the king of Israel." When I arrived home only a short time after my departure, I figured my wife would be astonished to see me; but again, it was me who was surprised. My personal belongings were already packed for the trip—as if she'd expected all long for the king to let me go! However, I knew I needed more than my personal belongings. This wasn't the first "prophet" I'd been to. I instructed my servants to pack up a load of silver, gold, and clothes to take with us as payment for, as they say, "services duly rendered."

I kissed my wife, and she gave me that same gentle squeeze. Just as I finished my goodbyes, the king's courier showed up with a sealed letter addressed to Joram, King of Israel. I held tightly to the scroll, mounted my horse, and turned my gaze to my wife's eyes. How did she know? How did my wife know the king would allow me to go—and immediately? Unconsciously my lips formed the word in my mind, "How?" She softly spoke one word, "Faith."

Faith? Faith in what? Faith in whom? I turned my horse towards Samaria, Israel's capital city, and supposedly the location of this prophet. Samaria is about a hundred miles south and west of Damascus, and a good three-day journey. That gave me some time to think.

I kept mulling over the changes in my household. I couldn't avoid the plain truth: ever since that girl came to live with us things were different. First, my wife seemed happier. Our arguments were now almost always one-sided—my side. The idols disappeared, yet she said she prayed. To what or to whom, I didn't know. I never heard of praying to some unseen God. And then to top it all off this "faith" thing. What was that all about? I couldn't make sense of it, but I found myself feeling the faintest tickle of hope rising inside of me. Maybe this time would be different. Maybe—faith, I've never tried that before. But faith in whom...this prophet-man?

Three days later we entered Samaria and the home of King Joram. To say there was a buzz around town was an understatement. People stepped back with fear and scrambled to get out of the way as my entourage and I rode through the streets and headed straight for the palace, entirely skeptical of this faith thing. However, I was curious to hear what Joram would say. Of course, we were given immediate access to the king. Wasting no time, I motioned my courier to hand the letter to the king. Suspiciously, Joram slowly broke the seal and began to read. As was customary for King Ben-Hadad, he was frank and to the point. He wasted no words, "When this letter reaches you, know that I have sent to you Naaman my servant, that you may cure him of his leprosy."

And he brought the letter to the king of Israel, which read, "When this letter reaches you, know that I have sent to you Naaman my servant, that you may cure him of his leprosy." And when the king of Israel read the letter, he tore his clothes and said, "Am I God, to kill and to make alive, that this man sends word to me to cure a man of his leprosy? Only consider, and see how he is seeking a quarrel with me." (2 Kgs. 5:6-7)

You'd think Joram saw a ghost! He turned white as sheet and thought this was some kind of extravagant hoax to start another war. He lamented, "Am I God, to kill and to make alive, that this man sends word to me to cure a man of his leprosy? Only consider, and see how he is seeking a quarrel with me." I'd seen fear in countless men's eyes as they watched my sword plunge towards them. They knew death was their close companion. I recognized that same fear etched upon King Joram's face.

But when Elisha the man of God heard that the king of Israel had torn his clothes, he sent to the king, saying, "Why have you torn your clothes? Let him come now to me, that he may know that there is a prophet in Israel." (2 Kgs. 5:8)

Nevertheless, he collected himself and whispered something to one of his aides who scurried out of the room. Joram called for a dinner to be fixed, and we were quickly ushered into the banquet hall where musicians and jesters entertained us. Joram was stalling for time. He was a worthless coward. How in the world this people followed him was beyond me. But, I let it go. I was tired from the journey and hungry. I may as well eat before I kill him, I mused.

An hour or so later, when we were eating, Joram's aide returned and whispered something into his ear. A grin broke out on the king's pitiful face. Although I was unable to hear the message, it is recorded in verse eight; apparently, the Israelite prophet, spoken of by my slave, knew of my search and sent word for me. His name was Elisha. The note read, "Why have you torn your clothes? Let him come now to me, that he may know that there is a prophet in Israel."

Joram stood up and proudly announced that I was to go to this prophet, this man of God named Elisha, and he would cure me. What a fake Joram was, I thought. It's good his father was king before him, because he never would have amounted to anything on his own. But, I'd heard enough. I didn't travel over a hundred miles to go chasing around after some no-count prophet. I decided to head back. I told my lieutenant to ready the horses for the return trip. Unfortunately, my lieutenant was also my nephew; and as you may guess, he was my nephew on my wife's side. He pulled the old "uncle" card on me and convinced me to follow through. In that moment, I knew I would break my wife's heart if I didn't at least see Elisha, so I played along and instead of heading home we headed towards this prophet of God.

Joram was thrilled to see us go. It was evident that he too was suspicious of this Elisha guy. Of course, I didn't understand it at the time, but Elisha held the true power, and Joram knew it. All I perceived in the moment were nuances of insecurity and jealousy oozing from Joram. That was enough to sweeten the pot for me though, and I committed to meeting the man who so skillfully undermined this idiotic king.

So Naaman came with his horses and chariots and stood at the door of Elisha's house. (2 Kgs. 5:9)

I led my entourage of horses and chariots out, and we headed for Elisha's home. We pulled up in the courtyard about thirty feet from the front door. I sat astride my mount, and surveyed the farm and ranch operation. Not very fancy, I thought, but efficient. I was told Elisha housed several men whom he was teaching. From the outside, one could see everything had a purpose. Everything was in order; this was a well-run operation. Elisha immediately gained my respect. I actually looked forward to meeting him.

After a minute or two, the door opened and out came a young man, hastily walking toward us. I assumed he was coming to take our horses and escort us into the house. Without regard to protocol, he walked past my lieutenant and addressed me directly. Clearly nervous, he looked up at me and said, "Go and wash in the Jordan seven times, and your flesh shall be restored, and you shall be clean."

The gall! Who did he think I was? Who did Elisha think he was? I was the commander of the army of Syria! I traveled over one hundred miles and he didn't have the basic courtesy to speak to me face-to-face? He sent some little runt to tell me to go take a bath in the Jordan River!

Once again, I was furious and let everyone know how I felt, "Behold, I thought that he would surely come out to me and stand and call upon the name of the LORD his God, and wave his hand over the place and cure the leper. Are not Abana and Pharpar, the rivers of Damascus, better than all the waters of Israel? Could I not wash in them and be clean?"

I reined my horse around in a rage and barked an order to my lieutenant. No other words were spoken. My men knew me well, and no one dared say anything.

And Elisha sent a messenger to him, saying, "Go and wash in the Jordan seven times, and your flesh shall be restored, and you shall be clean." But Naaman was angry and went away, saying, "Behold, I thought that he would surely come out to me and stand and call upon the name of the Lord his God, and wave his hand over the place and cure the leper. Are not Abana and Pharpar, the rivers of Damascus, better than all the waters of Israel? Could I not wash in them and be clean?" So he turned and went away in a rage. (2 Kgs. 5:10-12)

It was almost dusk. We road in silence for a couple of miles before pulling up to make camp. That evening I sat staring at the fire thinking. Just as the heat from the fire was leaving the last of the dying embers, so, too, my anger subsided. My nephew recognized that I'd cooled off some, and he decided to approach me. I must admit, the kid was pretty smart for someone younger than my own son. He used reason. He knew my pride and how I was gratified by my accomplishments, "Sir, if the prophet had told you to do something very difficult, wouldn't you have done it?" (NLT).

Of course, I would! Even with leprosy, I was more capable than most men half my age! I gave a substantial portion of my income to help the peasants. And heaven knows how much I gave to the temples and gods! I gained a lot in my life—wealth, fame, fortune, and respect!

But his servants came near and said to him, "My father, it is a great word the prophet has spoken to you; will you not do it? Has he actually said to you, 'Wash, and be clean'?" (2 Kgs. 5:13)

But my nephew continued trying to convince me, "Has he actually said to you, 'Wash, and be clean'?" It hit me like a stampeding elephant. It wasn't about what I could do it was "faith"! I had to answer the question: Was I willing to set aside my pride, humble myself, and have faith in the words this prophet spoke?

I sat there in silence. No other words were spoken. Slowly, my men dispersed not knowing my decision. The fire was completely dead. I stared up at the stars while the words of Elisha's servant ran through my mind. "You shall be clean. You shall be clean. You shall be clean."

Yes, yes, I would do it! I wanted to be clean. I believed I could be healed. The following morning, we got up and broke camp early. The Jordan was sixty miles due east, and I drove my men hard to reach it as quickly as possible. Two days later we arrived, and I went down into the river, seven times, just as I was instructed. And when I came up that last time, I looked at my hands and they were back to normal! I looked at my feet, and they were whole! I touched my fingers to my face and the skin felt soft and smooth, just like the skin of a little child! I looked at my reflection in the water and saw no more ugliness. I was clean! I was healed!

So he went down and dipped himself seven times in the Jordan, according to the word of the man of God, and his flesh was restored like the flesh of a little child, and he was clean. (2 Kgs. 5:14)

Naaman was a proud man. He was independent, and believed he needed no one. But Naaman had a burden. He had a terrible disease that was slowly eating away at him and would eventually kill him. Unable to stop the crippling effects of leprosy he became a desperate man, seeking any way to relieve his burden. The burden Naaman had, we all have. But, our burden is not leprosy, it is sin. In the Bible, the disease of leprosy is often used as a metaphor for sin.

There's no cure for sin. No amount of "doing" rids us of its grip. The Bible tells us that sin brings forth death and that the wages of sin is death. Sin is a death sentence.

However, the little conjunction "but" is a game changer. But God. The Bible tells us that God stepped into human history and provided a way of salvation from the devastating results of sin. Just like with the story of Naaman, God's way is *through faith*. God sent his only Son to become a man. God the Son came to earth, and took on human flesh in the person of Jesus Christ. God took our sin and put it on his own Son. When we, like Naaman were "dead in our trespasses" God made us "alive together with Christ." Salvation is by faith alone, apart from works. Have you placed your faith in Jesus Christ for salvation?

But God, being rich in mercy, because of the great love with which he loved us, even when we were dead in our trespasses, made us alive together with Christ...For by grace you have been saved through faith. And this is not your own doing; it is the gift of God, not a result of works, so that no one may boast. (Eph. 2:4-9)

2

THE LORD REMEMBERS

I'd like to tell you a story. You call it a "testimony." It's a story of how God worked in my life. I served as a priest in Israel under the Old Testament priesthood. You might be thinking that's a big privilege and responsibility. Well, I'll grant you that being a priest was both a privilege and a responsibility. But you're likely thinking of Israel's famous priests, especially the high priests, men like Aaron, the first high priest. Or maybe, you've got in mind, priests like Eli the high priest that mentored the prophet Samuel. Or perhaps, you thought of the great priest Ezra who led in the rebuilding of the temple after our return from Babylonian exile. These are three of the most famous priests in Israel's history.

The high priest was the top dog—if you will—of the priests. He was the top religious leader, the ultimate "go-between" between God and man. After the exile the high priest became more than a religious leader, he wielded political and social influence like never before.[1]

No, I wasn't a high priest. That job went to the eldest son of the high priest. Nor was I a priest on level with Ezra. The fact of the matter is, I was simply a common, every day, run-of-the-mill priest from the hill country of Judea. There were hundreds of us at any one time, serving all across Israel.

You might recall that priests come from the tribe of Levi. Levi was the third of Jacob's twelve sons, born to him by his first wife Leah. Every priest was from the tribe of Levi, but not all Levites were priests, there were qualifications.

Daily routines consisted of offering sacrifices, serving as judges or mediators when there was a civil dispute between parties, and teaching people from the Old Testament scriptures. Also, we were responsible to maintain the temple, keep the incense burning, change out the bread, keep oil in the lamps, and other such tasks. These duties seem rather boring and mundane, especially to children. It doesn't sound like a job that little boys dream about. But that's the furthest thing from the truth. The truth be told, that's what every boy wanted to be when he grew up—or at least among us Levites!

Then Moses stood in the gate of the camp and said, "Who is on the Lord's side? Come to me." And all the sons of Levi gathered around him. (Exodus 32:26)

When you think of an Old Testament priest don't think about some wishy-washy, namby-pamby, spineless, soft-spoken old man. Are you kidding me! We'd play priest and robbers when we were kids. See, the priests were also in charge of protecting the offerings brought to the temple. Ezra mentioned this in his book. Ezra put twelve priests in charge of more than eleven million dollars' worth of gold!

But, one of my favorite stories about Levites is recorded in Exodus. Remember when Aaron led the people to make a golden calf and worship it? When Moses came down and discovered what was going on and he said, "Who is on the Lord's side? Come to me." Do you know who responded? It was the Levites! Moses then commanded that they strap on their swords and make quick work of those who refused to follow the Lord. These were the stock of men that priests were made of!

My name is Zechariah. No, not that Zechariah, I didn't write the book of Zechariah. There are thirty-nine men named Zechariah in the Old Testament. It was a pretty popular name for young men in Israel; even one of Israel's kings was named Zechariah. Another Zechariah served in the temple during the reign of King David. The last Old Testament prophet slain was named Zechariah. But I wasn't any of these famous Zechariahs. In fact, the Old Testament was completed by my time. Malachi, the last book in the Old Testament was written almost four hundred years before I lived. My story is recorded in the New Testament. In Luke's Gospel, chapter one.

In the days of Herod, king of Judea, there was a priest named Zechariah, of the division of Abijah.(Luke 1:5a)

I'm what you might call a "tweener," not a preteen, but a person who lived between the Old and New Testaments. Rome ruled the world and set up local authorities that answered to the emperor. Our local authority was a fellow by the name of Herod. Herod was full of himself. He called himself "Herod the Great" and demanded the title of "king." Herod the Great served Rome from 37 to 4 BC. In case you're wondering, yes, he was the guy that commanded all Jewish baby boys to be killed in an attempt to kill the baby Jesus. [2] He started what became known as the Herod dynasty. Several Herods from this dynasty are mentioned in the

New Testament. Anyway, that's how Luke introduces me, as a priest living in the days when Herod ruled, of the division of Abijah. I'll explain that division thing in a little bit.

But there I am, A priest named Zechariah. Unlike a lot of people, I've always liked my name, even as a child. I liked it because of the heritage, not only are there many famous Zechariahs in the Bible, but because we had a linage of them in my family. Yes, I liked my name and I planned to name my first boy Zechariah, but things didn't go as planned. The older I got the more I realized many of my dreams and plans didn't work out like I expected. Zechariah means "Yahweh remembers"[3] or *the Lord remembers*—remember that! It seems my name was more significant to me and my life story than I realized.

And he had a wife from the daughters of Aaron, and her name was Elizabeth. (Luke 1:5b)

My story isn't just about me; I was married, and any married man knows that life changes after marriage. Life's no longer just about you, there's a family to think about. My wife's name was Elizabeth. O, my dear Elizabeth. Her father was also a priest. It was like a pastor's son marrying the daughter of another pastor. Elizabeth and I knew each other since childhood. We even attended the same synagogue.

Of course, I didn't pay much attention to her until we were teenagers. I was more interested in playing with her brothers. In fact, I hardly knew my buddies had a sister until one day I went to visit my good friend Zadok when Elizabeth answered the door and wow! At the sight of her, something in me stirred and I could hardly speak. I stuttered and stammered around, making a fool of myself, but she just smiled and went and got Zadok. I mentioned to Zadok how pretty his sister was, and he just laughed. Zadok then spun around and said sarcastically, "I'll go tell her for you." I tried to stop him but he was too quick. I turned and bolted, running all the way back home.

And they were both righteous before God, walking blamelessly in all the commandments and statutes of the Lord. (Luke 1:6)

Well that's how it started. Before long Elizabeth and I were the talk of our little village. Soon after we started seeing each other we knew we'd marry one day. We made plans; we both wanted a large family. She had four brothers and two sisters, and I came from a family of six boys. We married, and I completed my studies and became a full-fledged priest. Both of us worked hard and honored the Lord in all we did. I'm not bragging, just giving you the context for what follows. Luke said it this way, "...they were both righteous before the Lord."

After a couple years we moved to a village where I served the people of the small community. A small-town priest didn't make much money. We had a little house and Elizabeth sewed dresses and made children's clothes to help with the family income and to keep busy. With the little bit of extra money, Elizabeth made baby clothes and set them aside. She'd show them to me and I'd say, "Is that for little Zechariah?" She'd nod her head and smile.

So there we were: good, godly folks, serving the Lord, living lives that honored him. But like I said earlier, things didn't go as planned. Little Zechariah never came, and the years went by. In fact, many, many years went by and no baby.

But they had no child, because Elizabeth was barren, and both were well advanced in years. (Luke 1:7)

After more than fifty years, all hope of having a child was long gone. Even now, I can still recall those first years of marriage. We had dreams and hope. We dearly wanted children. We prayed for weeks, months, and years. But after several years we'd given up hope. At first I was mad at God. Why? We'd done everything the "right" way. My anger turned to self-pity. I have to admit, Elizabeth handled it better than I did.

A priest was supposed to have all the answers. And I would. When someone asked why God allowed this, didn't prevent that, or was silent when prayed to, I'd give them some pious sounding cliché. They'd give me a disingenuous smile, turn and walk away. It made me feel empty like I'd lied to them. Then one day I was reading the ancient book of Job and the Lord spoke to me so clearly it seemed almost audible. Job too demanded an answer from God. Job was chewed up and spit out by Satan like no other man in the Old Testament. Job lost everything, his family, his wealth, and his own health. When God finally spoke to Job it was with questions. God asked Job a slew of questions, one after the other in rapid-fire succession. Job had no answer. When confronted by God, he was speechless.

"Who is this that darkens counsel by words without knowledge? Where were you when I laid the foundation of the earth? Tell me if you have understanding." (Job 38:2,4)

That was it. That's all I needed. Here's what I learned: God is smarter than me. I'm not all knowing, he is. Another passage, from the prophet Isaiah, became so much more meaningful. Isaiah wrote that God's thoughts and ways are different from our thoughts and our ways. In other words, we don't think like God thinks; and we don't act like he acts. His ways and thoughts are so far above ours they are incomprehensible to the human mind. That's where I left it. I didn't have an answer. God didn't clue me in. He didn't have to. He's under no obligation to me. When I understood that and accepted his sovereign lordship over my life I was freed to serve him without complaint.

"For my thoughts are not your thoughts, neither are your ways my ways, declares the Lord. For as the heavens are higher than the earth, so are my ways higher than your ways and my thoughts than your thoughts." (Isaiah 55:8-9)

Did all the hurt go away? No. Every time Elizabeth and I visited family it hurt. We had a passel full of nieces and nephews. But we'd never have our own, and it hurt.

So, there you have it, you're all caught up with my life when Elizabeth and I are introduced by Luke. We were having a good year, things were rolling along smoothly. Elizabeth was still sewing dresses and making children's clothes. Now, not so much for money but for ministry. I think she gave away more clothes to the poor than she sold to the more well-to-do folks.

As I mentioned earlier, I was a member of the Abijah division of Levites. Long ago the priesthood was divided into twenty-four divisions; each division served twice-a-year for one week in the temple. This particular week my division was on duty. We were responsible to take care of the routine duties in the temple. But, as it turned out, there were more priests than duties. So, we cast lots for the sacred duties. The sacred duties were the most desired.

Now while he was serving as priest before God when his division was on duty. (Luke 1:8)

One of the most prestigious duties was offering incense in the holy place. A priest was permitted to do this only once in a lifetime.[4] Every time my division was on duty, I prayed that I was selected, but the lot never fell on me, until this year! Talk about being excited and nervous! Even at my age I was somewhat nervous. This was a great honor.

According to the custom of the priesthood, he [Zechariah] was chosen by lot to enter the temple of the Lord and burn incense. (Luke 1:9)

At the proper time, I entered the outer courtyard through the north gate. There was only one gate leading to the temple proper, the gate called Beautiful. Upon entering the Beautiful gate, I walked through the women's court, and saw ladies all about kneeling in prayer. I found the same in the Court of Israel, where Jewish men were praying. Slowly, reverently, I walked past the brazen altar, toward the steps, which led into the Holy Place. I felt the eyes of the people on me.

And the whole multitude of people were praying outside at the hour of incense. (Luke 1:10)

At the top of the stairs, I paused, taking it all in. I was about to enter the Holy Place. Only priests were allowed entrance. This was a very sacred task, and not one to be taken lightly. I knew exactly how everything inside will be laid out. On the south wall, to my left, will stand a menorah with seven candles burning. On the north wall to my right will sit the Table of Showbread. Directly in front of me will be the Altar of Incense. This is where my duties will be carried out. When the incense burned, the people outside can see the smoke rising from the chimney, signifying the prayers of God's people ascending to his throne. Behind the Altar of Incense was a thick curtain that separated the Holy Place from the Holy of Holies. It is there, behind the vail, that the Ark of the Covenant once stood. The Holy of Holies was only entered once a year, on the Day of Atonement, Yom Kippur. Only the high priest was permitted to enter. He offered a sacrifice for himself and the entire nation.

I carefully pulled the large door open. A cool breeze swept over me from inside. Slowly I stepped in. Everything was as I'd pictured it, but even more amazing. Everything was immaculate. I smelled olive oil burning, keeping the menorah lit. Mixed with the smell of olive oil was the smell of burned incense. I felt an overwhelming since of unworthiness as I entered. Two other priests entered with me, they were tasked to replace the showbread and olive oil. They soon departed, and left me alone in the Holy Place to burn the incense.

What happened next took me by complete surprise. I thought everyone had departed so I didn't expect to find someone else inside, standing right next to the Altar of Incense. The sight of this massive figure about scared me to death, this was no priest. It took only a moment to realize this was no man! An angel of God stood in the Holy Place! They never told me about angels being in the Holy Place. Needless to say, I was greatly disturbed.

And there appeared to him an angel of the Lord standing on the right side of the altar of incense. And Zechariah was troubled when he saw him, and fear fell upon him. (Luke 1:11-12)

I was still trying to gather my wits when the angel spoke telling me not to be afraid and then started going on about my prayer being answered, Elizabeth having a son, and me naming him John. "Whoa, whoa, whoa, hang on a sec. Just slow things down," I thought to myself. I was still trying to take all this this in. My thoughts were scattered, racing through my mind, bouncing all over the place. I tried to sort things out. This didn't make any sense. I hadn't prayed for a son in decades, and Elizabeth was well past childbearing years. What did he mean, a son? Naming him John?

But the angel said to him, "Do not be afraid, Zechariah, for your prayer has been heard, and your wife Elizabeth will bear you a son, and you shall call his name John." (Luke 1:13)

But the angel just continued, like I should have expected his appearance, saying that I'll be joyful and glad. And that the child will be "great" before the Lord. Then the angel said the child will be filled with God's Spirit from birth and will be like the great Old Testament prophet Elijah. His mission in life will be to prepare Israel for their Lord.

> *"And you will have joy and gladness, and many will rejoice at his birth, for he will be great before the Lord. And he must not drink wine or strong drink, and he will be filled with the Holy Spirit, even from his mother's womb. And he will turn many of the children of Israel to the Lord their God, and he will go before him in the spirit and power of Elijah, to turn the hearts of the fathers to the children, and the disobedient to the wisdom of the just, to make ready for the Lord a people prepared."* (Luke 1:14-17)

I just stood there stunned. My mind began to clear a bit. My thoughts were beginning to organize. I began to process what I'd heard. My prayer for a son from years before was heard by God? Elizabeth was going to have a son? I'm to name him John? How shall I know this?

Okay, things were becoming clear. I was thinking straight again. I had a couple question for this angel, who made such lofty promises. Who does he think he is showing up saying we'd have a son? No. No, we won't; life was determined for us long ago. When I was young I was more optimistic. But for years life has gone on, one day after another. Nothing special. No big deal. Just the mundane, familiar beat of life's drum. Elizabeth and I settled in to a comfortable routine. We went about life's everyday business. Yes, just who was this angel guy? And how do I know he's being straight? I said as much, "How shall I know this? For I am an old man, and my wife is advanced in years."

> *And Zechariah said to the angel, "How shall I know this? For I am an old man, and my wife is advanced in years."* (Luke 1:18)

The answer I got wasn't what I expected. You might say he shut me up. He paused, as if surprised by my curt remarks. The imposing figure looked directly into my eyes and with slow measured words said, "I am Gabriel. I stand in the presence of God, and I was sent to speak to you and to bring you this good news." At that moment I feared for my life. I lowered my proud head in shame and listened. He continued, "And behold, you will be silent and unable to speak until the day that these things take place, because you did not believe my words, which will be fulfilled in their time." The angel suddenly vanished, and I was left alone in the Holy Place.

And the angel answered him, "I am Gabriel. I stand in the presence of God, and I was sent to speak to you and to bring you this good news. And behold, you will be silent and unable to speak until the day that these things take place, because you did not believe my words, which will be fulfilled in their time." (Luke 1:19-20)

What did I just do? I was a priest of the Lord, in the Holy Place, being addressed by the angel Gabriel and I doubted God's word. Many people in the twenty-first century claim they just need a sign from God and they'd believe. If an angel spoke to them, they'd listen. I beg to differ.

It was taking me longer than normal and the people outside were getting anxious, looking for the smoke from the incense to rise. The other priests waited outside the Holy Place for me to join them to offer the benediction. I quickly lit the incense, finished up, and hurried out to join the other priests. Finding my place in line, I held my hands up with the others to pronounce with them the benediction, but no words came out. After the benediction, several priests approached me and asked why I didn't join in with the benediction. I tried to explain using hand signs that I had seen an angel, finally they got the idea.

And the people were waiting for Zechariah, and they were wondering at his delay in the temple. (Luke 1:21)

That was that. I remained mute. I was unable to speak. *Me*— the guy with all the answers was speechless. I finished my week of duty in silence and headed home.

And when he came out, he was unable to speak to them, and they realized that he had seen a vision in the temple. And he kept making signs to them and remained mute. And when his time of service was ended, he went to his home. (Luke 1:22-23)

When I got back home I could tell that Elizabeth was concerned. It seems word of my experience in the Holy Place got back to our little town before I did. My, how quickly news spreads! But all she knew was that I went in, took longer than normal, and that I couldn't speak when I came out. When I got to the house I told—or should I say—I *wrote* down for Elizabeth what happened. Although, I saw she was surprised by what the angel told me, she seemed content, and rather pleased. I didn't know if she was more pleased she didn't have to listen to me for some months or that she was going to have a child. She was confident, and unlike me she didn't question.

It wasn't long and Elizabeth was pregnant. She kept it to

herself for as long as she was able, but after a few months it was hard to hide her condition.

After these days his wife Elizabeth conceived, and for five months she kept herself hidden, saying, "Thus the Lord has done for me in the days when he looked on me, to take away my reproach among people."(Luke 1:24-25)

When Elizabeth was six months along we received an unexpected visit from one of Elizabeth's nieces, you know her. Her name is Mary. Mary was also pregnant, she was three months along. When Mary came in, our little baby boy leaped inside Elizabeth with joy. Elizabeth had keen spiritual insight and knew Mary was carrying the Christ. But that's another story.

After nine months, just as Gabriel said, we had a son. Elizabeth and I were once again the talk of the town! Folks came from all over our little village to celebrate with Elizabeth. What a great time that was! Everyone was talking, praising God, and bringing baby gifts. Most of the time, I just sat there watching, taking it all in with a big smile on my face. Not much else to do, I still wasn't able to talk! And I don't need to tell you how all those women were fusing over Elizabeth and the baby.

Now the time came for Elizabeth to give birth, and she bore a son. And her neighbors and relatives heard that the Lord had shown great mercy to her, and they rejoiced with her. (Luke 1:57-58)

After a couple days things settled down a bit as Elizabeth and I were trying to adjust to having a baby to care for. According to the

Old Testament law all Jewish boys were to be circumcised on the eighth day after their birth.[5] It was also tradition to name the boy on that day. Meticulous records of Jewish births, especially boys, were kept in anticipation of the promised Christ through the linage of King David. So, on the eighth day after our son was born, Elizabeth and I went to a fellow priest to have our boy circumcised and his name entered in the official records. Of course, this was another big deal and again, the whole town seemed to have showed up for the event.

Living in a small community everyone knows your business. Worse than that they all want in on the action. When we arrived for the procedure Elizabeth was asked what the boy's name will be. The town's people took it upon themselves and answered for her, "Zechariah, call him Zachariah after his father" they yelled to the priest. In one sense, that did make me feel good, some of the older folks recalled how years ago I dearly wanted a son and to name him Zechariah.

And on the eighth day they came to circumcise the child. And they would have called him Zechariah after his father. (Luke 1:59)

But it didn't sit right with Elizabeth. I think she was a bit put off by the people's presumptuous conclusions. She emphatically voiced her son's name, "No; he shall be called John." I think she offended some of them! Or at least confused them, some even questioned her choice, "None of your relatives is called by this name." They weren't going to let it lie so they turned to me. Surely, I'd straighten out my wife and give the boy a proper name. A name to be proud of. A name that meant something. They made hand signs to convey their message. I don't know why, I was mute, not deaf. I knew they wanted me to overrule Elizabeth. "What did I want?" they asked.

But his mother answered, "No; he shall be called John." And they said to her, "None of your relatives is called by this name." (Luke 1:60-61)

By now I too was getting a little agitated and motioned for a writing tablet, in big letters for all to see I wrote, "His name is John." There was a collective sigh in the room like I'd written a curse word! But, that put a lid on it. They didn't understand, but they accepted my word as final.

And they made signs to his father, inquiring what he wanted him to be called. And he asked for a writing tablet and wrote, "His name is John." And they all wondered. (Luke 1:62-63)

As soon as I wrote "His name is John" something happened. I knew my voice had returned and the first words spoken were words of praise to God. That got their attention! They hadn't heard me speak for nine months and when John was named, *bam*, my voice returned!

And immediately his mouth was opened and his tongue loosed, and he spoke, blessing God. (Luke 1:64)

Needless to say, that made for some commotion! They knew

something was special about John. They scattered like mice and spread the word through the countryside of Judea. They knew John was different, from his conception to his birth, he was a special child and there was no doubt that the hand of the Lord was with him. Everywhere the people went spreading the word, they questioned among themselves, "What then will this child be?"

And fear came on all their neighbors. And all these things were talked about through all the hill country of Judea, and all who heard them laid them up in their hearts, saying, "What then will this child be?" For the hand of the Lord was with him. (Luke 1:65)

That question stuck with me, "What then will this child be?" The name John originally comes from the Hebrew that means *Yahweh has graced. The Lord has graced.* No doubt Elizabeth and I were graced by the Lord with our son John. I believed there was more to it than that. But I never dreamed of how much more. Through the years the question kept coming back, "What then will this child be?"

It turned out John was a lot like me, he was quite the talker. In fact, that's what he was born to do, speak. Our son John was later distinguished by the addition of a name that described his ministry, *the Baptist.* Yes, I am father to John the Baptist. John was the forerunner of Jesus. It was John who was privileged to introduce Jesus to the world. As I said, John spoke a lot, but perhaps the most important words he ever uttered were captured by the Apostle John in chapter one of his Gospel. This is how my son, John the Baptist, introduced Jesus, "Behold, the Lamb of God, who takes away the sin of the world!" Yes, *the Lord has graced.*

The next day he [John the Baptist] saw Jesus coming toward him, and said, "Behold, the Lamb of God, who takes away the sin of the world!" (John 1:29)

∼

J ohn didn't live a long life, like the Lord that he proclaimed; John's life ended suddenly and violently at the hands of an unjust government. Perhaps that's another reason God waited. Elizabeth and I didn't live long enough to witness our son's cruel death; we were waiting to receive him in Heaven.

NO AVERAGE JOE

I'd like **to** tell you my story. You call it a "testimony." It's a story of how God worked in my life. I was just an "average Joe," you might say. In fact, that's my name, *Joe*. I grew up in a rather large family when compared to the twenty-first century American standard of 2.3 children per household. But in the first century BC, 8-10 children were rather normal for Jewish families. That's when I lived. But to better understand my life, you must have a little background information about my people, Israel.

Being a Jew wasn't easy back then. Then again, it's been pretty rough for the Jewish people ever since our exile to Babylon. That was 600 years before my time when the prophet Daniel and his friends were taken captive by Nebuchadnezzar. I can't say there's anyone to blame but ourselves. We were warned, but we didn't listen.

See, the Jews were a privileged people. God chose to send his promised Redeemer through us. This *Redeemer* was promised way back in the Garden of Eden when Adam and Eve sinned. The Lord, said his Redeemer would restore a right relationship between God and humanity. Ever since that dreadful day, in Eden when sin stained humanity, things started going downhill—fast! In fact, believe it or not, humans soon started making up their own gods to worship. Idol worship, it's called. Whenever worship to the true God is replaced by something else, it's called idol worship.

Abraham, the father of our people, was called out of an idol worshipping religion and was told he would be the father of *a great nation*. The funny thing was Abraham's wife, Sarah, couldn't have children! Well, God fixed that, and Sarah gave birth to a son when she was ninety years old! His name was Isaac. Isaac married a beautiful woman named Rebekah, but she too was barren. After twenty years, God opened her womb and she gave birth to twin boys, Esau and Jacob. Jacob had twelve sons. God changed Jacob's name to Israel and his twelve boys became the heads of the twelve tribes of Israel.

That's a brief history of how the nation of Israel and the Jewish people came into being. It's a miraculous history. A history that only God could have orchestrated.

Now the Lord said to Abram, "Go from your country and your kindred and your father's house to the land that I will show you. And I will make of you a great nation, and I will bless you and make your name great, so that you will be a blessing. I will bless those who bless you, and him who dishonors you I will curse, and in you all the families of the earth shall be blessed." (Genesis 12:1-3)

Remember I said that Abraham was promised to be the father of a great nation? Well, there's more to it than that, much more. Abraham was also told that in him *all the families of the earth shall be blessed.* "So, what does that mean?" you ask. Let me tell you. That's the promised Redeemer. The Redeemer of mankind will be through the nation of Israel. In fact, he will come through the tribe of Judah; Jacob's fourth son. What a privilege it was to be a Jew! God's chosen people. God's choice to bring about the redemption of humanity was promised to the nation of Israel.

Some ask why God chose Israel. In fact, this was the question that was on the hearts of the new generation of Israelites that God delivered from Egyptian bondage. Was it because Israel was so great? So big? So mighty? No, Moses addressed this when he wrote, "It was not because you were more in number...but it is because the LORD loves you." Israel was chosen because God chose the smallest, not the biggest. God chose to use the little, insignificant nation of Israel to bring his Redeemer into the world. But Israel had some issues.

"It was not because you were more in number than any other people that the LORD set his love on you and chose you, for you were the fewest of all peoples, but it is because the LORD loves you and is keeping the oath that he swore to your fathers..." (Deut. 7:7-8a)

Israel had two major problems: (1) a strong pull to worship a god of her own making; and (2) national pride. These two things caused so many problems for us. Like I said, there's no one to blame but ourselves.

Our first problem was worshipping a god of our own choosing. Recall that Abraham came from a religion that worshipped idols. Although the true God called us away from this type of worship and warned us not to go back, the pull was strong. Shortly after being freed from Egyptian bondage, what did we do? We built a golden calf and bowed down to it. Our second problem, our national pride, drove us to demand a human king just like all the other nations. Up until that point, God reigned as our King and placed judges, or prophets, over us to lead us. People like Moses, Joshua, and Samuel were all chosen by God to lead us even though they were never crowned king. But we didn't want God telling us what to do; we'd rather have another human calling the shots.

We selected Saul as or first king; that didn't work out so well. But God, in his grace, chose David to replace Saul. No doubt, David was our greatest king. But as generations passed, the monarchy produced more and more kings who led us to worship idols. This resulted in Israel being taken captive by the nations of Assyria and Babylon. The Babylonian exile ended the monarchy. But we've always looked for one more king. A king who would be our deliverer.

"When your days are fulfilled to walk with your fathers, I will raise up your offspring after you, one of your own sons, and I will establish his kingdom. He shall build a house for me, and I will establish his throne forever." (2 Chronicles 17:11-12)

I don't want to skip mentioning something about our great king, David. God promised David an eternal throne in Jerusalem. The Lord called it an everlasting kingdom. This kingdom would be established by a King anointed by God to sit on the throne of David, restoring Israel's prominence in the world. This anointed one, this "Messiah" (in Hebrew) or "Christos" (in Greek) translates to "Christ" in English. This one, this *Christ*, was the great hope of Israel. He would be Israel's Deliverer. That promise was made to King David a thousand years before my time, but even at my birth, the hope still lived in the hearts of Jews everywhere.

But you, O Bethlehem Ephrathah, who are too little to be among the clans of Judah, from you shall come forth for me one who is to be ruler in Israel, whose coming forth is from of old, from ancient days. (Malachi 5:2)

We haven't had a king since before the exile in 586 BC, nearly 600 years before I was born, but we knew the Christ would be a descendent of King David. That's why we kept careful birth records. We always lived in anticipation of the Christ. In addition to being a descendent of David, the prophet Malachi said the Christ would be born in Bethlehem, that's where King David was from.

That brings us back to me. My family is originally from Bethlehem; and I'm a descendent of King David. No, no, I'm not the Christ; not by a long shot! I'm just an "average Joe," born one of many children. Our family left Bethlehem and settled down in the region of Galilee, in the little village of Nazareth, where I worked the family trade as a carpenter. Times were tough. There wasn't much money, and the family business struggled just to keep in the black. Nevertheless, life went on.

I did the best I could to help mom and dad make ends meet. When my brothers knocked off for the day, I'd stay working, getting the job done so we could collect the payment. Mostly, payment came in the form of trade. We'd get vegetables, maybe some olive oil, and occasionally even a lamb or a side of beef for our services. It wasn't much, but we survived.

Mom, like most moms, was overly concerned for me. All my brothers, both older and younger, were already married, and there I was, single, working overtime every day, living in a back room of the family house. I didn't have time for a wife much less a bunch of little ones running around. My best friend, Benjamin, was always trying to introduce me to this girl or that girl ever since he married. It's not that I didn't think about being married, I was just so busy all the time.

Until one day I was stopped in my tracks.

As usual, I was working in the shop when a customer came in to order some shelves. Dad usually dealt with the customers; I filled the orders by doing the hands-on labor or supervising my brothers. I wasn't much of a people person. Maybe that's why I was still single. Anyway, dad was busy with another customer and he called me up front to take the gentlemen's order. I came in from the workroom and introduced myself to the gentleman. With him was a lady, who I thought was the gentleman's wife. Her back was turned to us, and she was looking at the tables and chairs on display. While the gentleman was explaining what he wanted, the lady turned and came to his side. I suddenly realized this wasn't his wife, but must be his daughter. And boy was she a looker; and just a few years younger than me, I presumed.

She had a pleasant smile. It was an innocent, shy type of smile. I immediately wondered if she was married. Why would I do that? Why would I care? I was too busy. I had too much to do. I took the man's order; it would be an easy order to finish. I told him I could deliver it in a couple days, after the Sabbath day.

Why did I do that? We don't deliver unless requested and then at an extra fee. But I volunteered to deliver—for free. Why? Maybe because I thought if he came back to pick-up the order he'd not bring his daughter. Silly. Why would I care? I was too busy. I had too much to do.

I had the work completed the next day. Should I deliver it so soon? Would I seem over anxious? What was I talking about? And why was I talking to myself? She probably didn't even care. She hadn't said a thing except, "Shalom" when she was leaving. But that was just the common Jewish greeting meaning peace. No, I'd wait. It was Friday, and the next day was the Sabbath. I'll take it over after the Sabbath day, the next week, like I promised.

I couldn't get her out of my mind. To say I was preoccupied was an understatement. Mom sensed something was wrong when I didn't finish my meal. "What's the matter?" she asked. "Are you sick?" Well, I was feeling a little queasy—stomach turning, dry mouth, nervous. But I don't think it was any sickness that herbal tea or a physician could fix.

As usual, we went to synagogue on Sabbath. In synagogue, the men and women sat separately. I found myself looking towards the women and children when I saw her looking my way. Her eyes quickly went down and I hastily looked to the front and listened to the scriptures being read; or at least acted like I was listening. After the service, I went outside with the other men when I saw mom talking to, of all people, the girl! "Joseph, come over here please," mom said. "I'd like you to meet someone. This is Mary." Yea, I'm *that* Joe; *Joseph, the husband of Mary* as Matthew describes me in his Gospel.

It wasn't long and our families became great friends, and Mary and I were engaged to be married. Engagements in first century Judaism were much different than engagements in twenty-first century America. Back then, in Jewish culture, an engagement was as binding as a marriage license. The bride and groom would publicly state their commitment to each other and swear oaths of affirmation that were legally binding. The groom gave the bride presents and a date for the marriage ceremony was set.

Once the two were engaged, although they still lived separately, there was no going back. The only way out was an official writ of divorce. That being said, neither Mary nor I had any doubts. We were deeply in love, and we both looked forward to the day we'd be married. She, of course, continued living with her parents while I was busy building us a house in my spare time.

I didn't see Mary as much as I'd have liked to—between the

business and building a house—I kept busy. Mary kept herself busy teaching children at the synagogue school and helping to care for her nieces and nephews. In fact, we'd only see each other regularly on the Sabbath. After the worship service, our families would generally join for a large family meal. Following the meal, the children played games while the adults visited and talked politics and religion. Mary and I spent this time dreaming and planning our future. Of course, we planned on staying right there in Nazareth. I'd eventually take over the family business and raise any boys we might have to learn carpentry as well. It didn't provide a lot of money, but I figured carpenters would always have a job.

About four months after our engagement things unexpectedly and drastically changed—Mary suddenly disappeared without warning. I found out when I went to synagogue one Sabbath day. As usual, I arrived a bit early and was talking to the other men while keeping an eye out for Mary and her family. The service was starting, and they hadn't shown up. But this wasn't completely out of the ordinary. Occasionally, the whole family came traipsing in together like a herd of cattle in the middle of the second or third song and I'd see Mary, face beat-red from embarrassment.

Sure enough, at the beginning of the second song here they came, the whole clan. But no Mary. Mary was still missing by the time the scripture reading started. I wasn't too concerned. I figured she was sick or had to stay with a child who was. What hit me as strange was Mary's mother refused to make eye-contact with me. She just stared at the ground, tightlipped, the whole service. I sensed something was wrong. After the service, I caught up with Mary's father. He, too, was somber looking and his usual smile gone. Something was definitely wrong.

"Where's Mary?" I asked.

His head dropped as he uttered just two words, "She's gone."

"Gone? Gone where?" I asked.

"Judah, to her aunt's house," he said and hastily walked away.

I was stunned. Judah? That's a good eighty miles south on the other side of Samaria! What in the world took her to Judah, I wondered. And why the big haste? Why didn't she even say good-bye? What was going on? When I last saw her, everything was fine with not a hint of anything out of the ordinary. I needed some answers.

I ran to catch up with Mary's mother who was quickly heading for her house trying to avoid any contact. As she neared her door I yelled, "Wait, I need to find out about Mary!"

She stopped but didn't turn to look at me. I walked up behind her but she refused to turn and face me. She just kept her head down and softly muttered one word that shook my world apart, "pregnant."

Now the birth of Jesus Christ took place in this way. When his mother Mary had been betrothed to Joseph, before they came together she was found to be with child.... (Matthew 1:18)

She walked inside, and left me standing there. I was shocked into silence, contemplating that one word, "pregnant." Pregnant, Mary? No, I couldn't believe it. Not Mary. Or could it be? And with whom? Why? I was crushed.

I didn't go home that day or even that night. I went for a long walk out into the countryside. I walked passed the shepherds tending their sheep. It must have been a good five or six-mile walk before I was away from everyone. I didn't want to talk, eat, sleep, or work. I wasn't sure if I even wanted to live.

Finally, I came to the edge of a small, natural, spring-fed pond. No one was around. With both hands, I picked up a large rock and heaved it into the water venting my anger. Why? Why did God do this to me? I had been faithful to him. I thought Mary was the one. Mom said Mary was the perfect wife for me. "Sweet, gentle, godly, everything a man could want," she said. Now it was over. All my plans were displaced like the water splashed from that little pond.

Suddenly, my thoughts began to whirl. What will I do? Who was this guy that dared to take advantage of Mary's innocence? Then again, Mary's mother didn't indicate that Mary was attacked or taken advantage of. Was this something Mary wanted? I know what most men in my position would do and even what I felt like doing. They'd make a spectacle of Mary. Bring her up on charges of adultery and have an open and public trial. Expose and shame Mary and the one responsible for her pregnancy.

No! I was hurting, but what will that prove? It may make me feel temporarily vindicated, but it wouldn't accomplish anything. It wouldn't be right. I still loved Mary and didn't want her to suffer any more than she had to. No; I'll not do this publicly. I'll discretely and privately divorce her. I'll free her to marry the other guy.

And her husband Joseph, being a just man and unwilling to put her to shame, resolved to divorce her quietly. (Matthew 1:19)

So, there I stood, considering these things. Broken hearted and staring into the pond, contemplating. The water had settled down and was as calm as when I first arrived. Would my life do the same, I wondered? Sometime, long after midnight, emotionally and physically exhausted, I drifted off to sleep. It was a restless sleep. I kept waking up with an expectation that all was well only to realize, afresh, my hopeless situation.

Mary told me she had never been with a man. She said she was a virgin and promised God to remain so until she married.

How did this happen? How did she go so wrong? Was I that naïve that I couldn't tell there was someone else?

I finally succumbed to fatigue and slept soundly. Then a dream came. An amazing dream where an angel appeared. He was a huge being, frightening in appearance, but he had a gentle spirit. His speech demanded an audience. He spoke with a clear, distinct, and booming voice of authority. I remember his exact words. He began with, "Joseph, son of David." I'd never been addressed as being the son of David; my father's name was Jacob. I knew I was being reminded of my heritage. Like I said, I was a descendent of King David, thereby a legal heir to the throne.

The angel continued, "Do not fear to take Mary as your wife." That was both encouraging and confusing. Encouraging because I still deeply loved Mary. Confusing because she was pregnant with a child that wasn't mine. That will complicate things, I thought. But what he said next was really going to complicate things far more than I ever imagined. The words of the angel changed my life like no other words. The angel said, "For that which is conceived in her is from the Holy Spirit."

Did I hear that right? God's Spirit caused Mary's pregnancy? Mary was still a virgin...yet she was pregnant? Two thousand years ago we didn't have the scientific technology you have today, but we knew it took a man and a woman—a male and a female—to make babies. A virgin didn't have babies.

While I was contemplating what was being said, the angel continued, telling me more about the child Mary was carrying, "She will bear a son, and you shall call his name Jesus."

But as he considered these things, behold, an angel of the Lord appeared to him in a dream, saying, "Joseph, son of David, do not fear to take Mary as your wife, for that which is conceived in her

> *is from the Holy Spirit. She will bear a son, and you shall call his*
> *name Jesus, for he will save his people from their sins."* (Matthew
> 1:20-21)

A son. Mary's baby will be a boy and I was to go through with the marriage. By going through with the marriage, I would legally be his father making him a legal heir to the throne of David. Even though Mary was also a descendant of King David, rights were passed down through the father. Of course, with the boy being conceived by the Spirit of God, who could argue his right to reign? Then again, who would believe how he was conceived?

His name was to be *Jesus.* Jesus was a Greek name, and the Hebrew equivalent of "Joshua." From the teaching at synagogue, I knew Joshua means "Yahweh saves"—*the Lord saves*—and the angel affirmed the meaning of this. Mary's son was going to be a Savior of his people, "For he will save his people from their sins" were the angel's exact words.

I didn't fully comprehend the implications of the child being a Savior at the time. When the angel said, "his people" I just assumed he meant Israel. What's worse, although I heard, I didn't understand the last part, "from their sins." I figured that meant the corporate sins of the nation. The common understanding was that the promised Messiah, the Christ, would lead Israel out of Roman bondage just as Moses had led Israel out of Egyptian bondage. We, as a nation, never really understood the full implications of "from their sins."

Still groggy, my head was spinning trying to take all this in. Was this real? Or was it just a hopeful dream I invented out of my depression? It seemed real. I never would have concocted such an unbelievable story. I wanted to believe it was real, yet I still had doubts. Then I recalled the words of one of our ancient prophets, Jeremiah I think. No, no, it was Isaiah. Isaiah wrote something to his generation about a young woman or maybe, a virgin, conceiving, having a son, and God being with his people. A virgin having a baby that was conceived by God's Spirit. That would be *God with us* would it not? Suddenly, I was fully awake.

It was a dream. But still, it was utterly real. I wanted to believe it. I wanted to believe Mary was innocent. I wanted to believe I could still marry her in good conscience. But I needed confirmation. God's Word. I'd go there. It was Sunday, the first day of the week. I needed to go to the synagogue where a copy of the scriptures was kept. I hoped to find someone there that would grant me access to the scrolls. With a renewed spark in my step, I walked back to town; arriving just after sunup.

The town was waking up as I walked through the avenues in the coolness of early morning. People began filling the streets heading out to set up for market or to make a trade or purchase. Normally a friendly town, the people didn't greet me as they usually did. In fact, they avoided me. They averted eye contact and crossed the street to escape me. Those that did catch my glance lowered their head and slowly nodded as if to say, "I'm sorry." The word was out. The whole town knew Mary was pregnant and she hastily left town.

I felt anger rising inside, but then I thought, what were they to think? Could I blame them? I'd have thought...in fact, I did think the same thing. No, I'll not hold it against the town's people; they've been good to me and my family. They just didn't understand.

Finally, I arrived at the synagogue and banged on the door until the president of the synagogue opened it with a start, "What's going on, where's the fire?" he complained with a broad smile on his face.

"Sorry," I said.

"Well good morning Joseph. How are you this lovely day?"

By his demeanor, I could tell he hadn't heard the news yet. It seems our priest was always the last to know. "I'd like to look at something from scripture, if you don't mind," I asked. He was happy to accommodate me. It wasn't often when a young man came by to seek answers from scripture. Usually young people sought the advice of their friends. How smart was that?

I told him what I was looking for and he pointed me to Isaiah. He wasn't exactly sure where it was, but he knew the passage I was speaking of and said it was early in the book. Isaiah was a long book, so I was happy he at least knew the general location. I started reading at the beginning. Skimming more than anything, I stopped abruptly when I came across the passage I was searching for. It's in what has been since designated as chapter seven, verse fourteen: *Therefore the Lord himself will give you a sign. Behold, the virgin shall conceive and bear a son, and shall call his name Immanuel.*

Could this be? No. Or could it? Immanuel means *God with us.* Yes, yes! After reading scripture I was convinced that Mary's pregnancy was from the Lord. It made sense. And it explained a lot! Mary *was* true to her character. She hadn't been unfaithful. She had remained a virgin, yet was pregnant. Why didn't she just tell me? But I quickly chastised myself knowing I never would have believed it without the angel. I could hear her now. "Hi, Joe. How was your week? Oh, by the way I'm pregnant but don't worry, I'm carrying God's Son."

It was obvious that her parents didn't believe her and were ashamed of their daughter. That was the reason she went to visit Elizabeth. Elizabeth was Mary's favorite aunt. Mary always talked about how Aunt Elizabeth and Uncle Zechariah told her Bible stories. Mary believed they were the godliest folks on earth. Come to think of it, I recall something about Aunt Elizabeth being pregnant with her first child, and she was an old lady! And, not only that, but rumor had it that old Uncle Zechariah became mute after having some vision in the temple. Now it makes perfect sense why Mary would leave and go to visit Elizabeth.

Well, you know the story. I went on to wed Mary. She remained a virgin until after she had her first child. When she returned from Judah, I accepted her with welcome and open arms. She was pleased, but the rumors around town didn't stop. In fact, rumors about her miraculous conception followed us our whole lives. It seems most of the town's folk never did believe.

After a few more God-controlled events, Mary's baby was born in Bethlehem. We named him Jesus, just as I was instructed. The promised one Israel had been looking for was God himself—God the Son—Jesus Christ. Now, looking back, I have complete under-standing, *for he will save his people from their sins.* Who would have thought that God would use an average Joe to raise his Son?

Matthew records that Joseph was told Mary would have a Son conceived by the Holy Spirit and he was instructed by the angel to, "call his name Jesus, for he will save his people from their sins." Who are Jesus' people? Jesus tells us, "I am the good shepherd. I know my own and my own know me, just as the Father knows me and I know the Father; and I lay down my life for the sheep" (John 10:14-15). Jesus laid down his life for his people. Just as the angel proclaimed, Jesus *will save his people from their sins.* Everyone has sinned. Jesus is the promised Redeemer, God the Son, who took on flesh, was virgin born, lived a sinless life, and offered himself as a sacrifice acceptable to God as payment for our sins. Thereby reconciling us back to the Father. Jesus' payment for sin is offered to us by God's grace as a free gift, through faith in Jesus Christ.

4

THE GREAT CONSPIRACY

*P*eople love conspiracies. A conspiracy is a scheme, a plan, a plot to deceive. To hide truth. To mask reality. To distort facts. Conspiracies intrigue us. The greater the cover-up the greater the intrigue. I was part of the greatest conspiracy in human history—the conspiracy to hide the resurrection of one called Jesus the Nazarene.

I'd like to tell you a story. It's my story. You call it a "testimony." It's a story of God working in my life. My story is found in the New Testament gospels.

I was a soldier in the greatest army the world had ever seen—the army of Rome in the first century AD. On direct orders from Pilate, I was charged to guard the tomb of Jesus. But an unexplainable thing happened, and the body of Jesus disappeared. Seized with fear, three other elite Roman soldiers and I dropped like dead men. When I came to, I reported the missing body to the Jewish chief priests (Caiaphas and his father-in-law, Annas) that requested the tomb be secured with Roman guards.

After the Jewish leaders considered my report, they produced a large sum of money and told me to keep quiet about what happened. I was instructed to pay the others off and to report a lie about what transpired. We were told to say that someone stole Jesus' body while we slept.

And when they had assembled with the elders and taken counsel, they gave a sufficient sum of money to the soldiers and said, "Tell people, 'His disciples came by night and stole him away while we were asleep.'"(Matthew 28:12-13)

So that's what I did. I followed orders. That's what soldiers do. But this lie haunted me day and night for the rest of my life. I'd like to share with you the story surrounding this sinister lie.

For several years, I was a common legionary or soldier in Rome's army. Yes, I saw combat and plenty of it. I saw a side of humanity most refuse to acknowledge. I knew how cruel humans could be.

I hate to admit it, I was part of such cruel treatment. Even when I knew it wasn't right. In war, things become foggy. Right and wrong seem to lose their definition, and black and white turns to shades of gray. But I carried out my orders without question. When told to jump, I jumped. When told to stand still, I stood still. When told to whip a prisoner, I whipped. I was good at my job because I carried out orders, and for this, I was rewarded.

My centurion saw that I obeyed unquestioningly and promoted me to *optio;* that's equivalent to the rank of sergeant. It's a Latin word that means "to choose." It's where the English word *option* comes from.

The promotion made my wife happy How could it not? My pay doubled, and I had more control over my schedule. But, along with my pay, my responsibilities also increased. And I was no longer one of the boys. I was now a supervisor. When an officer issued an order, it was my job to see to it that the soldiers obeyed the order.

I was stationed in the providence of Judea where Pontius Pilate was the local governor. A governor or *prefect* was a ruler appointed by the emperor. No self-respecting soldier wanted anything to do with Pilate. He was a weasel, and after a pathetic attempt at being a Roman military man, he was making himself into an even sorrier excuse for a governor. Word had it that his position was secured by family connections. It certainly wasn't based upon innate ability. I was happy he was headquartered in Caesarea, and I was in Jerusalem.

Rome was the world power and nations were subject to her rule. Israel was one of these nations. Pilate governed the Judean people who recognized Jerusalem, not Rome, as their capital. Most were Jews, and they pretty much kept to themselves. They had their own religion that governed every aspect of their life. They also used their own courts, which took care of both civil and criminal matters in everything short of a capital offense—one in which a person could be sentenced to death. So, all Pilate had to do was keep the peace.

Life was good for a Roman soldier living in Jerusalem. We were more of a police force than an occupying army. Our job was to make the governor look good and quickly put down any uprising that even remotely smacked of treason against Rome. Although none of us liked him, we made spineless Pilate look good.

Pilate was a self-absorbed politician through and through. He'd check to see which way the political winds were blowing before making a decision. He was jumpy, scared of his own shadow, and paranoid that someone wasn't going to like one of his decisions. He often complained to Rome, and got his critics fired. All too often, things deteriorated because of his lack of leadership. We squelched more than one small riot to regain control of a situation that should never have gotten so out of hand.

That's the way things were when I found myself smack-dab in the middle of the biggest conspiracy the world has ever known.

Through contacts in the Jewish community, I learned that the Jewish Sanhedrin (that's Israel's highest court) had held a secret, middle-of-the-night trial. They voted to put to death a popular religious figure—Jesus the Nazarene. Jesus was found guilty of blasphemy under their religion; that is, claiming to be God.

Then the high priest tore his robes and said, "He has uttered blasphemy. What further witnesses do we need? You have now heard his blasphemy. What is your judgment?" They answered, "He deserves death." (Matthew 26:65-66)

Up to this point, I didn't know much about Jesus. Oh, I had heard the name. He was a prominent teacher of religion in the area. But I was Roman—a Gentile—and wanted nothing to do with the Jews or their religious beliefs. I figured everyone worshipped his own gods in his own way. The Greeks had their own gods, Zeus, Hermes, and Poseidon. I worshipped Roman gods such as: Jupiter, Mercury, and Luna. We Romans even took some of the Greek gods like Apollo. We figured the more gods the better. Besides, I wanted all my bases covered; and believe me, I needed my bases covered.

But the Jews, were a peculiar people. They worshipped only one God. That one God, they said, created and rules everything. No other gods. Just one. I admit, it made things a lot simpler, but it also made for one powerful God! Intelligent too! In fact, the Jews believed the one God they worshipped was all-powerful and all-knowing. Thinking about it—as I often did—it did make sense.

We Romans saw our gods more as "super-humans." They were essentially humans but with special powers. Similar to the Greeks, we regarded our gods as heroes and heroines. Like us, they had human passions, desires, and fallacies. But not the God the Jews worshipped. Israel's God, they said, is a *perfect* God. A *righteous* God. A God without sin. *Holy,* their scriptures say.

Anyway, the whole conspiracy started out as a simple Jewish religious trial. Jesus was accused of claiming to be God and that ruffled the feathers of the Jewish leadership. At first, I couldn't understand why they were so upset. He was clearly just some harmless, crazy guy like all the others who claimed to come from the gods. Then I thought maybe he was a power-hungry guy with an elaborate plan to deceive people into believing he was a god. But really, either way, he would soon be discovered and that would end it. Unless, of course, he *was* God. Then could they really kill an all-powerful God, without him allowing it?

Now the chief priests and the whole council were seeking false testimony against Jesus that they might put him to death, but they found none, though many false witnesses came forward. (Matthew 26:59-60a)

Jesus was becoming more and more popular with the Judean commoners and this posed a problem for the Sanhedrin, because his popularity threatened their authority. The Jewish people believed that a *Messiah,* or a *Christ*, one anointed by God to be King, was going to bring salvation to Israel. Some started to believe Jesus was this *Christ* sent from God. If he was their promised Messiah, that would mean *adios* to everybody who was somebody in Jewish life.

I was told the Jewish religious leaders were scheming for months, attempting to do away with Jesus. They tried to humiliate him publicly, but he always outsmarted them by beating them at their own game. They tried to trump-up charges against him, but no one could find where he violated any law—even their own religious laws.

Then, to top it off, reports began circulating, especially among the poor, that he had power to heal people. In fact, there were a couple stories that he raised people from the dead! Well, I found that hard to believe; but the stories were out there.

Hence, the Sanhedrin sought to silence Jesus once and for all. So, they brought charges against him and paid people to give false testimony, but they couldn't even get that right. Then the chief priest, who oversaw the whole kangaroo court, finally had Jesus trapped, or so he thought. The court produced two witnesses who claimed they heard Jesus say he would destroy their temple and rebuild it in three days.

At last two came forward and said, "This man said, 'I am able to destroy the temple of God, and to rebuild it in three days.'" And the high priest stood up and said, "Have you no answer to make? What is it that these men testify against you?" (Matthew 26:60b-62)

There simply was no case against Jesus in the Jewish court. So, Jesus remained silent. It was the accusers who had the burden of proof to make a case against the defendant. Jesus simply needed to remain quiet. And that's what he did, until he was questioned directly by the high priest. Caiaphas cut to the chase and demanded Jesus answer a direct question, "I adjure you by the living God, tell us if you are the Christ, the Son of God."

Then Jesus gave the high priest what he was looking for. In no uncertain terms, Jesus clearly claimed to be God, "You have said so. But I tell you, from now on you will see the Son of Man seated at the right hand of Power and coming on the clouds of heaven."

But Jesus remained silent. And the high priest said to him, "I adjure you by the living God, tell us if you are the Christ, the Son of God." Jesus said to him, "You have said so. But I tell you, from now on you will see the Son of Man seated at the right hand of Power and coming on the clouds of heaven." (Matthew 26:63-64)

It was at this point the high priest lost it. He tore his clothes, in a pious display of self-righteousness, and led the Sanhedrin to sentence Jesus to death.

Another problem for Jewish leadership was that Jesus was "found guilty" of breaking a religious law that Rome didn't care about. Remember, the Jews had the authority to fine, punish, and imprison under their own laws; but for capital offenses they had to appeal to Rome because only we had the authority over life and death. However, before Rome sanctioned an execution, a violation of Roman law that authorized a death sentence must be proven. Hence, in order for a Roman court to hear the case, the Jews needed to change the charges; and that's what they did.

Friday, the morning following their middle-of-the-night miscarriage of justice, the Jewish leaders brought Jesus to Pilate to stand trial in a Roman court. They intended to pressure Pilate into convicting Jesus of a crime punishable by death under Roman law. This is where my involvement in the conspiracy started. And I had a front-row seat. Like I said, for the most part, the Jews kept to themselves and handled their own civil and criminal matters. But this wasn't the case in the trial of Jesus, the Nazarene—they wanted Jesus dead.

When morning came, all the chief priests and the elders of the people took counsel against Jesus to put him to death. And they bound him and led him away and delivered him over to Pilate the governor.(Matthew 27:1-2)

Jerusalem was crowded with people from all over; it was the Jewish Passover week when Jews were required to come to their temple and offer a sacrifice. It was a time of excitement and festivity. Of course, Pilate was in town. It was a chance for him to play politics, endearing himself to the Jewish community. Extra Roman troops were brought to Jerusalem to help with security. Since I was stationed in Jerusalem, my men and I were assigned as the governor's personal guard.

It was early in the morning on that Friday when I reported to work and found the Jewish leaders waiting with their prisoner. Because the Jewish Passover began at six, the Sanhedrin wanted an immediate trial so they could continue with their celebration. I was already exhausted after overseeing the arrangements for a huge governor's feast to be held in just a few hours. Plus, as sergeant of the guard, it was my responsibility to ensure guards were in place before any court proceedings began; but with the added security demands soldiers were already working double-duty. So, I held over the nightshift for the trial. Needless to say, the soldiers weren't happy.

One soldier smirked, "How do you even know the governor will hold a trial?" I just looked at him and said, "It's Pilate." He sighed and rolled his eyes in understanding. Pilate would bend to the will of the people.

In short order, everything was in place and Pilate, with his entourage, entered the court. He took his seat while his friends and family sat behind him, off to the left. Normally, such a large following didn't accompany the governor to a court proceeding, but this was different. This was an unplanned trial that had the whole town in an uproar. This was a big deal, and no one wanted to miss the excitement. And of course, Pilate loved an audience.

I appointed two guards to stand behind Pilate, one on each side, another couple guards to escort the prisoner, and several guards standing in a semi-circle creating a safe distance between the governor and the crowd. The rest of the men stood with their backs to the walls. Their presence helped to keep the peace. I stood behind Pilate's seated family where I could see the whole courtroom.

I scanned the area one last time before I called out for the prisoner to be brought in. "Silence! The proceedings will now begin. Let the prisoner be brought before the most honorable Governor Pilate."

The courtroom fell silent, and the side doors open. Then entered Jesus, his hands clasped together, tightly bound in leather and tied to a heavy chain around his waist. The crowd parted as Jesus walked through them with a soldier at each side keeping pace. As the trio turned to walk toward the governor, someone in the back of the courtroom yelled, "Crucify him!" Suddenly, the whole courtroom erupted shouting, "Crucify him! Crucify him!"

Pilate raised his hand. "Silence!" I shouted. Order was restored.

Jesus approached the front of the courtroom, and I was close enough to read the expression on his face. It wasn't what I expected. He was different from all the others that stood before a Roman court. I was accustomed to seeing fear. Some would visibly shake begging for mercy knowing their fate lie in the hands of the court. I was also familiar with seeing disdain. Prisoners stood in contempt knowing their fate was sealed. They'd lash out with verbal assaults against their accusers or spit at the crowd.

But not Jesus. He remained silent. He didn't seem angry or even excited in the least bit. There was a quiet calm about him. He exuded control and I thought I almost sensed contentment—certainly peace. It was out-of-place and definitely out-of-character for a man facing execution. He looked up at Pilate and I could tell Pilate was shaken.

Pilate quickly looked away from Jesus and instead addressed the man's accusers, "What's the charge?" The high priest replied, "We found this man misleading our nation and forbidding us to give tribute to Caesar, and saying that he himself is Christ a king." Like I said, they had to change the charge against Jesus. The Sanhedrin found him guilty of blasphemy by claiming to be God. But that wouldn't fly in a Roman court. So, the charge became treason against Rome, which was a crime punishable by death. They accused Jesus of claiming to be King of the Jews.

Then the whole company of them arose and brought him before Pilate. And they began to accuse him, saying, "We found this man misleading our nation and forbidding us to give tribute to Caesar, and saying that he himself is Christ, a king." (Luke 23:1-2)

Pilate surveyed the mob before him. He was in a position he didn't like. The Sanhedrin brought him a man they claimed committed treason, but they had no evidence. There were no witnesses. Just a mob demanding his crucifixion. There's no way this would be right under Roman law, and Pilate knew it. But if he didn't go along with the Jews, they'd complain to Rome and it would look like he couldn't govern. Pilate, still clearly intimidated by the calm of Jesus, looked back to him, "Are you the King of the Jews?" A hush fell on the courtroom. Jesus' response was clear and succinct, "You have said so."

Now Jesus stood before the governor, and the governor asked him, "Are you the King of the Jews?" Jesus said, "You have said so." (Matthew 27:11)

Pilate commanded the prisoner taken to a room where he could question the accused in private. Pilate's only hope was for Jesus to afford him a way out through confession. Maybe Jesus would provide witnesses to prove his innocence. I had the guards escort Jesus up the stairs and to a back room where Pilate and Jesus could talk privately. I ordered the guards to wait outside, and personally escorted Jesus into the room. Pilate was pacing the floor, anguish written on his face. I stopped just inside the door while Jesus continued to the middle of the room before he stopped and waited. Pilate continued to pace. Jesus remained silent.

Earlier, during the trial, Pilate's wife gave me a message to deliver to her husband when I got the chance. I figured the time was as good as it would get to break more bad news to Pilate. I must admit, I was somewhat pleased to relay the words. "Sir," I said, "I have a message from your wife."

"Well, what is it?" Pilate barked back.

I walked over so Jesus couldn't hear. Pilate stopped his pacing and I whispered just loud enough for his ear, "Your wife said, 'Have nothing to do with that righteous man, for I have suffered much because of him today in a dream.'" Pilate closed his eyes and clenched his jaw. Now, on top of everything else, his wife was haunted by dreams that Jesus was a righteous man. I walked back to my position by the door. Pilate went back to pacing.

For he knew that it was out of envy that they had delivered him up. Besides, while he was sitting on the judgment seat, his wife sent word to him, "Have nothing to do with that righteous man, for I have suffered much because of him today in a dream." (Matthew 27:18-19)

I found the whole ordeal quite odd. Jesus was the only one who seemed to have his senses about him. The Jewish leaders and crowd were out of control triggered by anger and hate. Pilate was worried sick he might make an unpopular decision and jeopardize his position. And there stood Jesus, just as calm as if he was waiting in line at the market.

Finally, Pilate stopped pacing long enough to question Jesus. He obviously hoped, perhaps desperately, that Jesus would help him out of his dilemma, *"Do you not hear how many things they testify against you?"* Jesus didn't say a word. He just stood there. Pilate shook his head in disbelief, "Why will you not saying anything? Don't you care if you die?"

Then Pilate said to him, "Do you not hear how many things they testify against you?" But he gave him no answer, not even to a single charge, so that the governor was greatly amazed." (Matthew 27:13-14)

The questioning of Jesus went on for several minutes, but rather than getting the answers he was searching for, Pilate became even more frustrated. When he realized he wasn't getting anywhere with Jesus, Pilate commanded the prisoner be taken back out while he conferred with his advisors. I called for guards to return Jesus to the courtroom but stayed behind and listened to the plan devised behind closed doors.

Pilate had one more card to play. In a ploy to win the hearts of the Jews, each year at the governor's feast Pilate allowed the Jews to select a prisoner that he would pardon and release. Pilate used this as a display of power and mercy to gain popularity. This year, he would change things. He decided to select the most despicable prisoner and let the people choose between him and Jesus. "Barabbas!" I heard one of his advisors declare.

A sinister smile spread across Pilate's face. The malicious Barabbas was already convicted of murder and treason against Rome and sentenced to crucifixion this very day. Barabbas was hated by the Jews. Although I thought Pilate was a weasel, I must admit he came up with a seemingly foolproof plan to get Jesus released and to save face.

Now at the feast the governor was accustomed to release for the crowd any one prisoner whom they wanted. And they had a notorious prisoner called Barabbas. (Matthew 27:15-16)

With renewed confidence, Pilate and his band of advisors headed back to the courtroom. I led the way and again called for silence when we reentered the room. Once again, the restless crowd became silent in anticipation of Pilate's decision. He stood before the crowd and with an air of superiority stated his decision. It was really no decision. He was simply going to let the people decide for him—what a politician! Pilate asked the crowd, "Whom do you want me to release for you: Barabbas, or Jesus who is called Christ?"

So when they had gathered, Pilate said to them, "Whom do you want me to release for you: Barabbas, or Jesus who is called Christ?" For he knew that it was out of envy that they had delivered him up. (Matthew 27:17-18)

The people remained silent. They didn't expect this. They wanted a guilty verdict and the pronouncement of a death sentence. Caiaphas and his council conferred with each other while the crowd looked on and waited. Pilate watched. The Jewish leaders appeared to come to a consensus; they turned and whispered to the people closest to them. Those, in turn, whispered to the ones behind them, and so on. Soon the whole crowd was murmuring. But still, no answer from the people.

Pilate, growing impatient, asked again which prisoner was to be released. It wasn't the one he expected. "Barabbas!" the crowd shouted. "Release Barabbas!" Shocked, Pilate didn't know what to do. What was he going to do with Jesus, whom he knew to be innocent? Again, the spineless Pilate let the people decide, "Then what shall I do with Jesus who is called Christ?" Do something I thought! Take a stand. Do the right thing! But Pilate refused to make a decision. He let the crowd dictate what he would do with Jesus, "Let him be crucified!" Panic began to etch its way onto Pilate's face. His plan was backfiring. The crowd continued shouting. Pilate raised his hands and over the chant of the crowd said, "Why, what evil has he done?" The cry became even louder, "Crucify him! Crucify him!"

> *The governor again said to them, "Which of the two do you want me to release for you?" And they said, "Barabbas." Pilate said to them, "Then what shall I do with Jesus who is called Christ?"* (Matthew 27:21-22)

The mob continued shouting for the crucifixion of a man without evidence of wrong doing. I surveyed the crowd looking for anyone who might get out of control. I've seen this type of mobthink before. As I watched, my mind was racing, trying to rationalize what I was witnessing. Pilate's question haunted me. I couldn't get it out of my mind, "What shall I do with Jesus who is called Christ?" What would I do? Who was this man?

> *They all said, "Let him be crucified!" And he said, "Why, what evil has he done?" But they shouted all the more, "Let him be crucified!"* (Matthew 27:22b-23)

The people were on the verge of rioting. Even as I mulled the bizarre proceedings over in my mind, the military discipline drilled into me over years of training was kicking into autopilot. I signaled to my men and they circled around Jesus, keeping the crowd at bay. Pilate was already preparing a hedge to distance himself from the mess he made of the trial. He had one of his servants bring a wash basin to him. In front of the crowd, Pilate washed his hands and announced, *"I am innocent of this man's blood; see to it yourselves."* The people had no problem taking responsibility, and they voiced it, *"His blood be on us and on our children!"*

> *So when Pilate saw that he was gaining nothing, but rather that a riot was beginning, he took water and washed his hands before the crowd, saying, "I am innocent of this man's blood; see to it yourselves." And all the people answered, "His blood be on us and on our children!"* (Matthew 27:24-35)

In one last ditch effort to save Jesus from crucifixion, Pilate ordered Jesus scourged. Scourging consisted of a severe beating with a cat-o-nine tails leather whip. Pieces of glass, bone, or metal were imbedded into the leather straps. When whipped, these imbedded pieces cut and dug into the skin ripping away the flesh. The beatings were so severe that some prisoners didn't survive. But this, too, failed to appease the people and Pilate delivered Jesus to be crucified. Barabbas was set free and Jesus was turned over to the execution squad.

> *Then he released for them Barabbas, and having scourged Jesus, delivered him to be crucified.*(Matthew 27:26)

Fortunately, I wasn't part of the execution squad. It was bad enough overseeing Jesus' scourging. Again, I was amazed at his silence. I saw pain and suffering in his eyes as the whip ripped the flesh from his back. Every time the strap found its mark he winced; yet, not a word crossed his lips. Finally, it was over. When I gave the order to my men to deliver Jesus to the execution squad they were appalled. Even these hardened Roman soldiers saw the injustice and cruelty being done.

A different breed of men comprised the execution squad. Heartless and cruel. I often wondered whether cold-blooded and merciless men were selected for this squad or if being part of the execution squad turn men into ruthless killers. Whatever the case, the only relief for a prisoner from their brutality was death itself.

These men usually began their torture with the humiliation of the prisoner. I think this helped ease their conscience. As though killing a fool who broke the law warranted a complete erasure of their human dignity. And, as if on cue, that's where it started with Jesus. After mocking and making fun of him they headed toward a hill aptly named *"Place of the Skull."* I was relieved that our job was complete.

As I watched the heartless crowd leading Jesus and two other prisoners to their death, Pilate's question again crossed my mind, "Then what shall I do with Jesus who is called Christ?" Why were these words stuck in my mind? Soon Jesus would be dead. Everything would be done. No more Jesus *to do with.*

A few hours later the report came back to Pilate that Jesus was dead.

When it came to prisoners sentenced to death, that was usually the end of it for me and my men. Our responsibility ended with the handoff to the execution squad. But just like Jesus was different in his life, he was different in his death. He was more than some common Jewish man, or even a Jewish religious figure. For some reason, the Jewish leaders were afraid that Jesus' followers were planning an elaborate scheme to steal his body and claim he resurrected from the dead. There was even rumor that these followers were going to assert that Jesus came back to life and then ascended into heaven—alive. Caiaphas and his cronies said Jesus claimed he would come back to life after three days, and they wanted to stop any conspiracy by his followers to fake a resurrection. So, they requested Pilate assign Roman guards to the tomb.

> *The next day, that is, after the day of Preparation, the chief priests and the Pharisees gathered before Pilate and said, "Sir, we remember how that impostor said, while he was still alive, 'After three days I will rise.' Therefore order the tomb to be made secure until the third day, lest his disciples go and steal him away and tell the people, 'He has risen from the dead,' and the last fraud will be worse than the first." (Matthew 27:62-64)*

I thought the idea was rather foolish. I didn't see any of Jesus' supporters at his trial. If these disciples of his were brave enough to steal the body and claim he came back to life, why didn't they testify for him at trial? Pilate looked for any excuse to release him. Had his disciples, even just a couple of them, come forward during Jesus' questioning, Pilate likely would have suspended judgment against him. It made no sense to me. I would have refused their request. But I wasn't Pilate.

> *Pilate said to them, "You have a guard of soldiers. Go, make it as secure as you can." So they went and made the tomb secure by sealing the stone and setting a guard. (Matthew 27:65-66)*

Guess who was tasked with setting the guard? You guessed it, yours truly. When I told my men of our assignment they were understandably upset. These were proud Roman soldiers, not grave keepers. But the grumbling stopped when I told them Pilate authorized extra pay for volunteers. Suddenly everyone wanted to ensure the body of this dead man stayed in its tomb.

I split the watch into four six-hour shifts and assigned four soldiers to each rotation. Because of the religious laws governing these people and their contact with anything dead, the first shift didn't need to begin until after the Jewish Sabbath ended at six pm on Saturday. No self-respecting Jew would touch a dead body during Sabbath–even a Jew intending to steal that body. I decided to put myself on the second shift. I figured midnight to six would be the quietest shift and we'd finish up right at sunrise before people were out and about. Boy, was I wrong!

It was still dark, not quite six am, when the guard I assigned to the outside perimeter called out, "Hey, Sarge, I've got some ladies here that want to visit the tomb." "Escort them in," I responded.

Now after the Sabbath, toward the dawn of the first day of the week, Mary Magdalene and the other Mary went to see the tomb. (Matthew 28:1)

The other two guards and I stood as the ladies walked toward us escorted by the perimeter guard. Suddenly, the earth shook and a blinding light flashed across the sky! The light descended to where we were and appeared as a massive figure of a man. But this was no man. He stood at least a foot taller than any man I had ever laid eyes on, and he was so bright he glowed. I grabbed my shield to cover my eyes and instinctively unsheathed my sword. The massive being single handedly pushed the stone away from the tomb. That's all I remember. Fear, like I've never known, came over me. My legs gave way—and everything went black.

And behold, there was a great earthquake, for an angel of the Lord descended from heaven and came and rolled back the stone and sat on it. His appearance was like lightning, and his clothing white as snow. And for fear of him the guards trembled and became like dead men. (Matthew 28:2-4)

I felt kicking at my side, "Sarge, are you okay?" Things were still a bit fuzzy when I came to. Soldiers from the dayshift arrived to find me and the other three guards passed out, the stone rolled back, and the tomb empty.

"What happened? Where's the body?" one of the soldiers asked. "Were you over powered?" he asked.

"Yeah, I'd say so," I replied. I ordered the four dayshift guards to conduct a thorough search of the perimeter in every direction for two-hundred yards. "What are we looking for, Sarge?"

"A body. Any evidence that someone dragged a body. Any sign that anyone was around. The night crew and I are going back to make our report to Caiaphas." With that, we headed back to town. I went immediately to the Jewish temple and demanded an audience with the chief priests.

I recounted the story to the leaders, just like it happened. The earthquake, the light, the massive figure, the stone rolled away, and the body gone.

"Did you see him—the body?" they asked. "No. No, I didn't see anything after the blinding light and the man, or whatever it was, rolled away the stone. None of us did. We passed out. Now my men are scared to death Pilate will have us executed for losing our prisoner...I mean our *body*," I said.

They assured us we'd be okay, and they'd take care of things with Pilate. They just wanted us to keep quiet. The priests handed me a heavy leather bag. "Here take that, divide it up with your men," they said. I looked into the bag, and saw it was filled with silver coins. I looked back at the priest who handed me the bag. He said, "Tell people, 'His disciples came by night and stole him away while we were asleep.' And if this comes to the governor's ears, we will satisfy him and keep you out of trouble."

While they were going, behold, some of the guard went into the city and told the chief priests all that had taken place. And when they had assembled with the elders and taken counsel, they gave a sufficient sum of money to the soldiers and said, "Tell people, 'His disciples came by night and stole him away while we were asleep.' And if this comes to the governor's ears, we will satisfy him and keep you out of trouble."' (Matthew 28:11-14)

I didn't like it. I had half a mind to go directly to Pilate and report the whole thing. But then I thought of my men. Pilate could hardly be trusted to make sound decisions. And in this case specifically, he was more interested in saving face than serving justice. Besides that, what if the Jewish leaders turned on me after learning that I spoke with Pilate? What would become of my men? I also had a wife and children to think about. I decided to take the money and keep my mouth shut. I was a good soldier, and I followed orders. But something inside me began to change.

I told the other three about our new orders and gave them their money. They were still clearly shaken by what we witnessed —whatever it was. I dismissed them to go home. When they were leaving, one soldier turned and asked, "Hey, Sarge, if we were asleep when Jesus' disciples came and stole the body, how do we know what happened?"

I shrugged my shoulders and shook my head. Again, Pilate's question came back to me, *"What shall I do with Jesus who is called Christ?"*

So they took the money and did as they were directed. And this story has been spread among the Jews to this day.(Matthew 28:15)

~

That's the question we all must answer, *"What shall I do with Jesus who is called Christ?"* Pilate refused to make a decision. He let the crowd dictate what he would do with Jesus. What about you? What's your decision?

5

BITTER TO THE END

I was a bitter man. Perhaps life as a career soldier contributed to my bitter spirit. Combat, violence, and death were common to me—more common than I'd like to admit. More than one man died at the end of my blade. I was good at my job. In fact, I was the best. There was no better military strategist. I had an uncanny ability to read men and strike a preemptive attack.

In warfare timing is critical, and I understood when the time was right. I knew how to bide my time—when to wait and when to attack. Understanding men meant I knew their strengths and their weaknesses. I didn't always fight fair, but I always fought to win—and win I did. In warfare winning is the only option.

But what about life, you might ask. My theory was that life presented two types of people: winners and losers—I wasn't a loser. My passion for winning spilled over into every area of my life. I didn't just win, I crushed my enemies. A dead enemy is a harmless enemy, in war, or in everyday life. When family and friends suggested my obsession with winning was unhealthy, I'd laugh it off and tell them I was simply a *driven* man.

Yes, I thought of myself as *driven,* or perhaps *determined,* or maybe even *ambitious.* But never *obsessed.* Obsession suggested I wasn't in control, but *driven, determined,* and *ambitious* are positive words! I believed I was in control of my destiny not *obsessed!* Are you kidding me!

I'd like to tell you a story. It's my story. You call it a "testimony." It's a story of God working in my life. I served in the army of Israel under Israel's greatest king, King David. I'll start with a little of my family and background before the army.

My name is Joab and even as a young boy, I dreamed of growing up and being a soldier like my famous uncle. My story is recorded in three Old Testament books: Second Samuel, First Kings, and First Chronicles. I was one of three boys; my brothers were Abishai and Asahel; our mother was Zeruiah; our dad was Suri.[1] We were from Bethlehem, a little village in Judah. Yes, *that* Bethlehem where a thousand years after my day, Jesus was born.

My family lineage, on my mother's side, is recorded in First Chronicles chapter two. If you are wondering why my father's family isn't given, it's because mom came from an incredibly important family. Mom had several brothers and a sister. Her father, my maternal grandfather, was Jesse. I don't like to brag, well, maybe I do, but Grandfather Jesse had seven sons. His youngest son was David—King David. Yes, my Uncle David was Israel's greatest king.

I'm listed in King David's genealogy with my two brothers Abishai and Asahel. But there's also one of my cousins listed: Amasa. Amasa played an important role in my later life.

Jesse fathered Eliab his firstborn, Abinadab the second, Shimea the third, Nethanel the fourth, Raddai the fifth, Ozem the sixth, David the seventh. And their sisters were Zeruiah and Abigail. The sons of Zeruiah: Abishai, Joab, and Asahel, three. Abigail

bore Amasa, and the father of Amasa was Jether the Ishmaelite.
(1 Chronicles 2:13-17)

I have fond memories of my early childhood. My brothers and I were inseparable. Being so close in age, we grew up playing, hunting, and fishing together. Not only did we share a passion for outdoor activities, but we all three shared a passion for soldiering. Coming from a shepherding family, we found lots of time to hone our weaponry skills while tending sheep.

Uncle David wasn't much older than us, and we regarded him more as an older brother than an uncle. In fact, we tended sheep with him before he became famous for killing Goliath. David taught us to use the bow, spear, sword, and sling. As you might have guessed, David was partial to the sling. He was amazing with it. I recall one fall when he killed a lion, and the following spring, he slew a bear; each one with a rock from his sling! But the most amazing thing about David was his quiet confidence. I envied his calm and confident demeanor. David could detach himself from the violence that seemed to follow him wherever he went. On the other hand, I was never able to successfully separate myself from the violence in my life.

I often caught David quietly meditating or writing. "Come on David, let's practice sword fighting!" I'd say to him. "In a little bit," he'd reply. "I'm busy now." I just couldn't figure my uncle out. He was so unassuming. If I hadn't personally witnessed his skill and courage, I'd have thought he was some harp playin', poetry lovin' sissy. But David was a different breed of man. My motto was: you cross me—you paid. I didn't leave room for forgiveness in any of my interactions. He, on the other hand, employed compassion and a forgiving spirit.

So Saul said to his servants, "Provide for me a man who can play well and bring him to me." One of the young men answered, "Behold, I have seen a son of Jesse the Bethlehemite, who is skillful in playing, a man of valor, a man of war, prudent in speech, and a man of good presence, and the LORD is with him." Therefore Saul sent messengers to Jesse and said, "Send me David your son, who is with the sheep." (1 Samuel 16:17-19)

Saul reigned during those early years. He was Israel's first king and the first to raise a standing army. As a nation, we saw our share of war, but Israel never had a standing national army since conquering the land under Joshua's leadership. My dream of being a soldier looked pretty good at the beginning of Saul's reign when the army mustered some 3,000 men. However, it quickly dwindled down to only 600. I was afraid there'd be nothing left by the time I was old enough to join.

Shortly after killing Goliath, David left to fight for King Saul permanently. After David departed, my brothers and I were left to carry on without him. But he quickly became our inspiration. We couldn't wait to grow up and join the army serving under David.

We had contests with our handmade bows, spears, swords, daggers, and, of course, the sling. Abishai and Asahel were every bit as competitive as me. This competitive spirit led us to become especially skilled. My personal favorite was the dagger, because I liked close combat. We used wooden swords and daggers to train. Often, a fight would break out after one of our "friendly" competitions and Abishai and Asahel ganged up on me. Knowing their weaknesses, I had a mental edge over them and defeated them each time—either separately or together. It was during these early years that I realized how important the mind was in battle. My brothers had skill, but I had that little edge that put me over the top. I knew what they were thinking and when they hesitated, I struck.

Our desire to fight for Israel never faltered. And before I knew it, we grew into strong, competent, and skilled young men. To be honest, I'd put my brothers up against any man I knew. But in close, hand-to-hand combat, I could take either one or both. Unless, of course, Abishai used his spear. I hate to admit it, but my brothers were unbeatable in two areas: spear fighting and speed.

Abishai used a spear like no man I'd seen. It was like he became one with it. I swear, Abishai could split a hair at twenty paces! Not only that, he learned to use it to wield off attacks using both the sharp and the blunt end. When Abishai raised his spear, it was best to stay clear of him. You might think I'm exaggerating about Abishai's skill, but consider what is recorded about him. The Bible notes that Abishai killed 300 men in battle with his spear. I told you he was good!

Now Abishai, the brother of Joab, was chief of the thirty [chief men]. And he wielded his spear against 300 men and killed them and won a name beside the three. He was the most renowned of the thirty and became their commander. (1 Chronicles 11:20-21)

Asahel's specialty was speed. He could run like the wind. This was a great advantage in our day when most fighting was done afoot. Asahel had unbelievable endurance and never seemed to get winded. Although the least skilled fighter, he was by far the fastest of us three. The Bible also records his skill as *swift of foot as a wild gazelle.*

And the three sons of Zeruiah were there, Joab, Abishai, and Asahel. Now Asahel was as swift of foot as a wild gazelle. (2 Sam. 2:18)

So, there we were, all grown up and ready for battle when the most unexpected thing happened—*David deserted the army.*

After joining the army, David quickly made a name for himself. He was promoted to captain and married one of the king's daughters. David and Jonathan, King Saul's eldest son and war hero, were best friends. Everything was set for my brothers and me to join the army when things went terribly awry.

The king had it out for Uncle David and attempted to kill him. But with help from Jonathan, David escaped and fled into the wilderness with King Saul and his army in pursuit. This is when my brothers and I joined David. I didn't want to go against my king, but I knew my uncle's heart. David wouldn't flee without good reason. I figured if I were on David's side, I'd be on the side of right. That turned out to be a good call.

It was during that time, under the command of David, that I learned the art of war. I learned how to outsmart the enemy, how to use the terrain to gain an advantage, and how to beat a superior force. But mostly what I learned from David was how he trusted God for victory. David never stopped his habit of meditating or writing. Nor did he lack that quiet confidence, which I came to admire. But, I was no David. David trusted God for victory, but I was much more pragmatic—or, so I believed—I trusted me.

While there's no doubt David was a brave warrior, he was also a man with a quiet and gentle spirit. I was not. I was a man of violence and I used violence to achieve my desired end. I recall one night, after everyone turned in, I found David sitting next to a dwindling camp fire writing. "What are those? Strategic plans?" I asked.

He smiled, shook his head and said, "No, I'm writing a song."

"A song! Are you kidding me! Saul's army is encamped on the other side of those rocks and you're writing a song!" I exclaimed.

David looked up from his work and smiled, "Yes, Joab, I am."

"Why?" I asked, and tossed more wood onto the fire.

The flames danced in David's eyes while he contemplated an answer. "Well, I was thinking about all this fighting and how scary it is when death is so close that it feels like a shadow. Then the Lord called to mind the time when we used to tend sheep. Remember those days, Joab?"

I nodded my recollection. "Okay, I'm game. Read me what you have so far."

"Well, here's what I've written:"

> The LORD is my shepherd; I shall not want.
>> He makes me lie down in green pastures.
> He leads me beside still waters.
> He restores my soul. He leads me in paths of
>> righteousness for his name's sake.
> Even though I walk through the valley of the
>> shadow of death,
> I will fear no evil, for you are with me;
> your rod and your staff, they comfort me.
> You prepare a table before me in the presence of my
>> enemies;
> you anoint my head with oil; my cup overflows.
> Surely goodness and mercy shall follow me all the
>> days of my life,
> and I shall dwell in the house of the LORD forever.[2]

"Well good luck with that David!" I smirked; "I'm going to get some shuteye." Again, a sincere smile came across David's face, "Goodnight, Joab."

That was the difference between David and me. While the Lord was his Shepherd, I followed no one. When wronged, I acted. When wronged, I made things right. When wronged, I went for the kill. So, there you have it. David took matters to the Lord, but I took matters into my own hands. Let me give you an example. It comes from the first battle after David was crowned king over Judah.

As you probably know, America's bloodiest war was its Civil War. Civil war is the worst kind. Brother against brother, father against son, families split, and victory doesn't feel like victory when your loved one receives the business end of your weapon.

The decisive battle in the American Civil War took place at Gettysburg. It was a victory for the Union. The first battle recorded in the Bible, in which I was involved, was the decisive battle of Israel's first civil war. It was fought at the Pool of Gibeon half-way between where the two kings set up their thrones. The story is recorded in Second Samuel chapter two not long after David became king. As mentioned, when my brothers and I joined David, King Saul was pursing David, but he was also at war with the Philistines. Now, we might have fled from our king, but we weren't fleeing from our country. There were about 600 warriors, along with my brothers and me, who all swore loyalty to David. But we were all committed to Israel. So, while hiding from Saul we also engaged in secret guerrilla warfare against our common enemy: the Philistines. Sadly, even with our help, things went badly for Israel. King Saul and three of his sons, including Jonathan, were killed in battle leaving Israel with no king.

Years earlier, David was anointed by Samuel to succeed Saul on the throne. After Saul's death, David asked the Lord if he should go to Judah, which is in southern Israel. The Lord told him to go. So, David led the whole clan, all 600 men and our families to Judah. When we arrived in Hebron, David was crowned king of Judah. This wasn't a big surprise. It was the area where we grew up. Our hometown of Bethlehem was only about ten miles north of Hebron.

Judah was the largest of Israel's twelve tribes. But, mind you, not all of Israel was ready to abandon Saul's family. Abner, who was the commander of Saul's army, led the effort to keep the throne in Saul's family. Abner established Ishbosheth, a son of Saul by a mistress, as king over the remaining tribes, causing an immediate split. As you might imagine, things were tense. Like America was split North and South with two presidents, Lincoln and Davis—we, too, were split North and South with two kings, Ishbosheth and David.

But Abner the son of Ner, commander of Saul's army, took Ish-bosheth the son of Saul and brought him over to Mahanaim, and he made him king over Gilead and the Ashurites and Jezreel and Ephraim and Benjamin and all Israel. Ish-bosheth, Saul's son, was forty years old when he began to reign over Israel, and he reigned two years. But the house of Judah followed David. (2 Samuel 2:8-10)

The years under David proved that I was a capable military commander and strategist. Men eagerly followed me into combat. Furthermore, David could find no one more loyal than me to both my king and my country. He had several competent soldiers, but I was the one he chose to be his commanding general. Faithfully, fighting alongside me were my brothers, Abishai and Asahel.

After months of posturing and small skirmishes, the two armies finally met at a small, deep pool located at a place called Gibeon. On that fateful day, Abner brought his army south, and I led mine north until we were in a face-off. Neither side making a move. I was discussing strategy with my brothers and was about to call for an attack when Abner proposed a compromise.

Abner the son of Ner, and the servants of Ish-bosheth the son of Saul, went out from Mahanaim to Gibeon. And Joab the son of Zeruiah and the servants of David went out and met them at the pool of Gibeon. And they sat down, the one on the one side of the pool, and the other on the other side of the pool. (2 Samuel 2:12-13)

Abner sent an aide over with a message, *"Let the young men rise and compete before us."* Abner suggested each side select twelve men to represent their army. The twenty-four men were to engage in hand-to-hand combat with the winner deciding the battle. That suited me just fine, and I agreed to the challenge. I sent back my reply, *"Let them rise."*

Asahel volunteered to fight, but I told him no. His skills were not in close, hand-to-hand combat. I ordered my captain to find twelve capable volunteers willing to fight to the death. Thirty minutes later, a dozen men reported to me ready for battle. Each army sent out their representatives and combat quickly ensued. The twenty-four men fought valiantly, but the contest ended with no victor—and no man left alive. The bloody field was dubbed the *Field of Daggers!*

And Abner said to Joab, "Let the young men arise and compete before us." And Joab said, "Let them arise." Then they arose and passed over by number, twelve for Benjamin and Ish-bosheth the son of Saul, and twelve of the servants of David. And each caught his opponent by the head and thrust his sword in his opponent's side, so they fell down together. Therefore that place was called Helkath-hazzurim, which is at Gibeon. And the battle was very fierce that day. And Abner and the men of Israel were beaten before the servants of David. (2 Samuel 2:14-17)

As soon as the last man fell, I signaled for an attack. Abner was caught off guard, and we hit him hard. We relentlessly pressed until Abner realized his army was no match for our superior force and ordered a retreat. He made a beeline north to save what was left of his army. It's a day that I will never forget—but, not because we won the battle.

As Abner fled, I glanced at Abishai. No words needed to be exchanged. We were united in spirit and thought. Asahel met our look, gave a smile of conformation, and bolted like a wild gazelle after Abner who was running for all he's worth. We weren't about to let him escape unscathed.

And the three sons of Zeruiah were there, Joab, Abishai, and Asahel. Now Asahel was as swift of foot as a wild gazelle. And Asahel pursued Abner, and as he went, he turned neither to the right hand nor to the left from following Abner. Then Abner looked behind him and said, "Is it you, Asahel?" And he answered, "It is I." (2 Samuel 2:18-20)

Abner didn't get far before Asahel started closing in on him. Abner looked behind him and said, "Is it you Asahel?" Asahel called back, "It is I." Looking back, I must admit, Abner gave Asahel ample warning. Asahel was faster and stronger, but Abner was the more seasoned soldier. In many ways, Abner and I were alike. He too could read his opponent. He knew their weaknesses and struck when they least expected it. But this time, Abner warned Asahel twice.

Abner pled, "Turn aside to your right hand or to your left, and seize one of the young men and take his spoil." Asahel refused and continued his pursuit. Abner wasn't warning Asahel out of mercy, he knew if something happened to Asahel he'd have me to deal with. Again, Abner warned, "Turn aside from following me. Why should I strike you to the ground? How then could I lift up my face to your brother Joab?"

Asahel was a son of Zeruiah. We were cut from the same cloth. Concede victory? No way. It was all or nothing. We cower to no man. Asahel refused to turn aside, and *Abner struck him in the stomach with the butt of his spear, so that the spear came out at his back. And he fell there and died where he was.*

Abner said to him, "Turn aside to your right hand or to your left, and seize one of the young men and take his spoil." But Asahel would not turn aside from following him. And Abner said again to Asahel, "Turn aside from following me. Why should I strike you to the ground? How then could I lift up my face to your brother Joab?" But he refused to turn aside. Therefore Abner struck him in the stomach with the butt of his spear, so that the spear came out at his back. And he fell there and died where he was. And all who came to the place where Asahel had fallen and died, stood still. (2 Samuel 2:21-23)

The sight of my brother's body stopped our army in its tracks —*all who came to the place where Asahel had fallen and died, stood still.* The sight of Asahel caused the men to think. They realized

Abner was luring us into a trap. Abner was gaining the high ground giving his army a tactical advantage. Also, it was getting late, and the sun was going down as Abner assembled his troops and prepared to redeploy them. Wisely, my men stopped their pursuit. But I didn't care, and I didn't stop. I was enraged by the sight of my brother's lifeless body, and I continued the chase.

Abishai stayed with me as I passed the other soldiers and raced right to the front of the army. It wasn't good tactics, a sense of duty, or loyalty to the king that drove us. It was bitter anger. The men—loyal soldiers all—fell in behind us and followed me in my foolish quest. We pursued Abner until we came to a hill called Ammah.

That's when Abner stopped. His men were already at the top of the hill and had the upper hand. He formed his soldiers into an attack position and simply waited for us to continue our advance. Abishai and I stopped at the bottom of the hill and looked up at Abner and his army. It was nothing short of suicide to continue. He knew it, and we knew it.

Then Abner offered words of wisdom. Amid battle, he kept his wits about him and, for that, I respected him. Abner called down to me and asked three rhetorical questions; all that cut to the heart of the matter. "Shall the sword devour forever? Do you not know that the end will be bitter? How long will it be before you tell your people to turn from the pursuit of their brothers?"

But Joab and Abishai pursued Abner. And as the sun was going down they came to the hill of Ammah, which lies before Giah on the way to the wilderness of Gibeon. And the people of Benjamin gathered themselves together behind Abner and became one group and took their stand on the top of a hill. Then Abner called to Joab, "Shall the sword devour forever? Do you not know that the end will be bitter? How long will it be before you tell your people to turn from the pursuit of their brothers?" (2 Samuel 2:24-26)

This was the wisdom of a counselor. Rather than telling me what to do he asked questions. Asking questions was much less threatening. It made me think, it made me reevaluate my position, and it mercifully gave me a choice. His first question was, "Shall the sword devour forever?" The war had been going on for a long time. Would it ever end? In conflict that pits brother against brother, the only winner is death. It may not always be physical death; it may be death of a relationship. However, it is death none-theless.

His second question was, "Do you not know that the end will be bitter?" Nothing good comes from a power struggle within a family. When there's a winner, there must be a loser. Bitterness will remain no matter who prevails.

His third question was, "How long will it be before you tell your people to turn from the pursuit of their brothers?" In other words, "The ball's in your court. You can stop this right now." Although still seething with anger, Abner's words hit a cord with my men and they saw the futility of an up-hill assault. Resentfully, I told him as much, "As God lives, if you had not spoken, surely the men would not have given up the pursuit of their brothers until the morning."

And Joab said, "As God lives, if you had not spoken, surely the men would not have given up the pursuit of their brothers until the morning." So Joab blew the trumpet, and all the men stopped and pursued Israel no more, nor did they fight anymore. (2 Samuel 2:27-28)

I'd like to say I took Abner's wisdom to heart, but I didn't. That moment was a turning point in my life. Had I listened, my life would have taken a very different direction. But, I didn't listen; instead I allowed bitterness to control me. Rather than believing he was being honest, I suspected Abner realized that eventually I would prevail...I mean *we* would prevail—David's army would... this wasn't about me. Or, was it? Maybe it was. Maybe my life was all about me.

Yet, I realized charging up that hill would be suicide for me and my men. The day's battle was over; and I sounded retreat. But the loss of Asahel was the only thing I took away from my encounter with Abner.

The war drudged on, and David became more powerful while Ishbosheth became weaker. It was clear that soon Israel would recognize and accept David as king over all twelve tribes. Abner was no fool. He could see what was coming. Although Ishbosheth sat on the throne, Abner was the one with the real power in the north.

Unknown to me at the time, Abner sent a message to David seeking a truce. David took the bait and welcomed Abner with open arms even ordering a big feast for him and his entourage. I was on a campaign and knew nothing of the truce until I returned to Hebron from battle. Before I gave an after-action report to the king, one of my aides informed me that Abner had been in the city and I just missed him. The aide said Abner agreed to deliver all Israel to David with no more bloodshed. David agreed to the treaty and Abner departed in peace.

Just then the servants of David arrived with Joab from a raid, bringing much spoil with them. But Abner was not with David at Hebron, for he had sent him away, and he had gone in peace. When Joab and all the army that was with him came, it was told Joab, "Abner the son of Ner came to the king, and he has let him go, and he has gone in peace." (2 Samuel 3:22-23)

I couldn't believe it! Was David getting soft? Was he losing his edge? Didn't he realize what Abner was up to? Abner came to spy out our resources not to make peace—or at least that's the way I saw it! I spoke in private to the King, "What have you done? Behold, Abner came to you. Why is it that you have sent him away, so that he is gone? You know that Abner the son of Ner came to deceive you and to know your going out and your coming in, and to know all that you are doing."

Then Joab went to the king and said, "What have you done? Behold, Abner came to you. Why is it that you have sent him away, so that he is gone? You know that Abner the son of Ner came to deceive you and to know your going out and your coming in, and to know all that you are doing." (2 Samuel 3:24-25)

David wouldn't listen. He believed Abner was being straight. David told me it was done, and he already sent Abner away in peace. I was ordered to leave it alone, but I couldn't. This wasn't about peace between Israel and Judah. This was about what Abner did to my brother. I wasn't about to leave it alone.

As soon as I left the king's presence, I sent men to entice Abner back to the city. If David wasn't going to take care of matters, I would. I went to the city gate and waited. It wasn't long before Abner and his entourage crested the horizon and made their way back to where I waited. Abner greeted me with a smile and a customary bow. I returned the gestures and asked him inside the gate-guard's room, "I have a special message for you, my friend," I told him.

"Yes, Joab, what is it?"

"This is for Asahel!" I said, and thrust my dagger deep into his side.

Abner looked into my eyes as life drained from his body. His lips struggled to form words. Slowly, I removed my dagger from his gut and I heard a gurgled whisper, "Do you not know that the end will be bitter?"

When Joab came out from David's presence, he sent messengers after Abner, and they brought him back from the cistern of Sirah. But David did not know about it. And when Abner returned to Hebron, Joab took him aside into the midst of the gate to speak with him privately, and there he struck him in the stomach, so that he died, for the blood of Asahel his brother. (2 Samuel 3:26-27)

How did he know bitterness marked my life? I served David as commander of his army my whole life. Success? I had it. Position? I had it. Wealth? I had it. But all of it was wrapped in a bitter cloak of anger.

Abner was right. I died a bitter man. In another fit of rage.

Years later, David's son, Absalom, revolted against his father and attempted to overthrow the kingdom. David ordered that his son to be taken alive. Absalom was captured, but despite the order, I killed him. That was the last straw for David. He'd had enough of my antics and planned to replace me as commander with my cousin, Amasa. That's when I murdered a second time; this time it was my own cousin.

After David died, I sided with his son Adonijah to replace David as king, even though I knew David wanted Solomon to take the throne. From his deathbed, David warned Solomon about me, "You know what Joab did. He murdered two of my commanders. Don't let his gray head go to the grave in peace!"

Solomon became king, and when he learned I sided against him, he ordered my death. I fled to the court of the tabernacle and took hold of the horns on the brazen altar.

"Moreover, you also know what Joab the son of Zeruiah did to me, how he dealt with the two commanders of the armies of Israel, Abner the son of Ner, and Amasa the son of Jether, whom he killed, avenging in time of peace for blood that had been shed in war, and putting the blood of war on the belt around his waist and on the sandals on his feet. Act therefore according to your wisdom, but do not let his gray head go down to Sheol in peace." (1 Kings 2:5-6)

As I knelt there, with my bloodstained hands clutching the altar, I thought about my life. It was all about me. When someone crossed me, I eliminated them. I had no use for anyone that didn't see things my way. The words David wrote came to mind, "He leads me in paths of righteousness for his name's sake." Why didn't I follow that path? Because it was always about me and what I wanted. For me, life was a never-ending war. I was at war with everyone, my enemies (real or imagined), my king, my country, my fellowman, and even my God.

Would anyone mourn my passing? How would I be remembered? I prayed my children would not be like their father. Again, Abner's words came to mind, "Do you not know that the end will be bitter?"

Solomon was informed as to my whereabouts. "Joab has fled to the tent of the LORD, and behold, he is beside the altar," he was told. I knew the end was near. King Solomon gave the command, "Go, strike him down." One of the best palace guards Benaiah was sent to do the job. He ordered me out, "The king commands, 'Come out.'"

"No, I will die here." My last recorded words were words of defiance. Life was about me; so was my death.

When the news came to Joab—for Joab had supported Adonijah although he had not supported Absalom—Joab fled to the tent of the LORD and caught hold of the horns of the altar. And when it was told King Solomon, "Joab has fled to the tent of the LORD, and behold, he is beside the altar," Solomon sent Benaiah the son of Jehoiada, saying, "Go, strike him down." So Benaiah came to the tent of the LORD and said to him, 'The king commands, 'Come out.'" But he said, "No, I will die here." (1 Kings 2:28-30a)

This chapter ends on a sad note; that's what bitterness does to us. Joab lived with a "root of bitterness." Bitterness sprouts when a person rejects God's grace, *See to it that no one fails to obtain the grace of God; that no 'root of bitterness' springs up and causes trouble, and by it many become defiled* (Hebrews 12:15).

Joab's life stands in stark contrast to David's life. David not only obtained God's grace, but he extended grace to others.

Joab came to a turning point in his life. He was in a position to put a stop to the conflict, but he chose not to. Even after peace was made by David with Abner, Joab refused to submit his stubborn will.

Is there conflict in your life? Are you at odds with someone in your family? Someone you work with or go to school with? A friend? A brother or sister at church? *"Do you not know that the end will be bitter?"*

---

*Then Benaiah brought the king word again, saying, "Thus said Joab, and thus he answered me." The king replied to him, "Do as he has said, strike him down and bury him, and thus take away from me and from my father's house the guilt for the blood that Joab shed without cause. The LORD will bring back his bloody deeds on his own head, because, without the knowledge of my father David, he attacked and killed with the sword two men more righteous and better than himself, Abner the son of Ner, commander of the army of Israel, and Amasa the son of Jether, commander of the army of Judah." (*1 Kings 2:30b-32)

6

ALMOST PERSUADED

I was born into a royal family, or at least that's how we like to think of ourselves. My great-grandfather was Herod the Great. He's the one who started the Herod dynasty in 37 BC. Think of *Herod* as our family name. We're descendants of Esau, Jacob's brother (whose name was later changed to Israel). Although not direct descendants of Jacob, we Herods like to think of ourselves as Jews by religion. I'll admit, it was more for political reasons than anything else. Nevertheless, we made sure we were familiar with the customs and controversies of the Jews. We especially tried to keep up with their religious beliefs.

See, we were appointed governors (or kings as we Herods liked to be called) by Caesar over Jewish regions. And more than anything, we wanted to hold onto our power and position. So, we went to great lengths to keep the Jews from creating an uprising and disrupting the *Pax Romana*—the Peace of Rome. Hence, we figured that being Jewish by religion would put us in good graces with the Jewish people and help endear us to the populace we sought to please. Great-grandfather was always worried about others trying to overthrow his little kingdom. You're probably familiar with him: Herod the Great. He's the one who was visited by the Wise Men from the East who told him the King of the Jews was born. Great-grandfather ordered all baby boys, aged two and under, killed in an attempt to ensure no one would take his throne.

Speaking of baby boys and thrones, I'm the only boy in my family. I have three sisters, so naturally, I figured to be next in line for the throne. My name is Agrippa, and I was named after my father, King Herod Agrippa. Although father and mother lived mostly in Jerusalem, I lived and was educated in Rome alongside Caesar's children. I was born in AD 27, which was around the time the man called Jesus (King of the Jews, as Pilate called him) was crucified on a Roman cross. Rumor had it that this Jesus was the one born in Bethlehem who my great-grandfather tried to kill when Jesus was a baby.

I'd like to tell a story; it's my story. You call it a "testimony." It's an account of how God worked in my life. The story is found in the New Testament book of Acts. It was a tough time to govern the Jewish people, especially after the crucifixion of Jesus. A new religious sect arose among the Jews. They were referred to as "Christ-followers." Soon they were simply known as Christians.[1] Even before the death of Jesus, tension was mounting between Christians and the other Jews. In fact, it's believed Jesus was tried for religious differences by the Jewish court and then turned over to Pilate for crucifixion. After the death of Jesus and his reported resurrection, things seemed to spiral even more out of control.

With all this going on, father had a hard time keeping the peace. Whose side should he choose? After some thought, he sided with the traditional Jews who far outnumbered this new sect of Christians. To ingratiate himself to the Jews, father had the fisherman James, one of Jesus' original followers, killed. This delighted the Jews, so father ordered another fisherman named Peter arrested. This is recorded in Acts, chapter twelve. It was not long after this that my father died suddenly, suffering a terrible death—eaten by worms. This is also recorded in the Bible.[2]

About that time Herod the king laid violent hands on some who belonged to the church. He killed James the brother of John with the sword, and when he saw that it pleased the Jews, he proceeded to arrest Peter also. (Acts 12:1-3a)

Claudius, a good friend of mine, was Caesar at the time of my father's death. I was sure he'd appoint me king in place of my father, but to my surprise, he didn't. Perhaps it was because I was only seventeen, and he figured that with all the turmoil taking place in Palestine I wasn't ready. Instead, Claudius made the country a Roman providence and appointed another man as procurator, a type of official manager, over the entire region.[3]

However, just four years later when my uncle, another King Herod, died Claudius appointed me over the now vacant throne. So, at the age of twenty-one I became King Herod Agrippa II. In addition to my governorship, and perhaps more important, I was also in charge of the Jewish temple and manager of its treasury. Because I oversaw the temple, I could to appoint the high priest at will, and believe me I did! The Jewish people didn't like the idea that their high priest served at my whim, but it gave me a powerful political friend. That's where things stood when the Bible mentions me.

The Bible only records one incident in my life. At the time, I didn't think much of it, but it turned out to be the most significant event in my life and I never forgot it.

The incident occurred about ten years into my reign, around AD 58 or 59, as I recall. It had been some thirty years since the death of Jesus and the tension between Jews and Christians wasn't getting any better. In fact, things were getting worse. And, unlike my father, the Jewish people never really cared for me, so I had to make sure that I made all the right political decisions—as to not lose my throne. This was the situation when I made the trip to Caesarea to meet with Festus, the governor of Judea. I was accompanied by one of my sisters, Bernice.

Now when some days had passed, Agrippa the king and Bernice arrived at Caesarea and greeted Festus. And as they stayed there many days, Festus laid Paul's case before the king. (Acts 25:13-14a)

We discussed the incident over dinner. Bernice and I were ushered into the large dining hall. Servants stood against the walls, there was a large table set for four. Fetus took his seat at one end of the table, I sat at the other. Bernice was seated on to my right, across from Fetus' wife. The incident concerned a prisoner named Paul who was being held in Caesarea. Festus laid all this out to my sister and me. The Jews wanted Paul moved to Jerusalem to stand trial. However, Festus learned of an assassination plot against the prisoner. It seemed Jewish leaders never indented for Paul to arrive at Jerusalem to stand trial. But Festus wanted to see justice done. So, he, along with Paul's accusers, made the trip to Caesarea and heard the case there. After hearing the case, Festus determined the Jews had no evidence to convict Paul of anything.

When the accusers stood up, they brought no charge in his case of such evils as I supposed. Rather they had certain points of dispute with him about their own religion and about a certain

Jesus, who was dead, but whom Paul asserted to be alive. (Acts
25:18-19)

Festus finished his dinner and snapped his fingers to have his
plate taken away and motioned for another glass of wine. He
summed it up for me, "After all was said and done, they brought
no serious charges against Paul, like I supposed. Instead, the
dispute was about the man named Jesus, whom the Jews said was
dead, but Paul claimed was alive."

A servant also took my plate and I watched him pour me a
fresh glass of wine. I took a sip and thought about what Fetus said.
That was the big dispute? Whether or not Jesus, who was crucified
some thirty years ago, was alive? That's it? What were these religious leaders afraid of, a dead man?

Festus knew the Jews had no case. I looked back at him and he
continued, "I'm at a *loss how to investigate these questions, I asked
whether he wanted to go to Jerusalem and be tried there regarding them"*
(Acts 25:20). Moving Paul assured the safety of the prisoner.
However, Paul unexpectedly appealed his case to Rome. By doing
so he put Festus in a pickle—because Paul was a Roman citizen.
Under Roman law Festus was obligated to honor Paul's appeal and
forward the case to Caesar. Clearly exasperated by the whole situation, Fetus sighed, *"But when Paul had appealed to be kept in custody
for the decision of the emperor, I ordered him to be held until I could
send him to Caesar"* (25:21).

To say I was intrigued with the case is an understatement. I'd
made it a point to follow news surrounding Jesus. The fact that my
great-grandfather attempted to kill him and that my father killed
one of his followers only increased my curiosity about Jesus. Then,
it appeared, that this guy, Paul, picked up the reins and was
regarded as a major leader—if not *the* major leader—of these so-
called Christians. Making the case even more captivating was the

fact that Paul was a Pharisee, and had even arrested Christians and persecuted them before he switched sides. What made him switch? Why the change in Paul? I had to find out. I spoke up, *"I would like to hear the man myself"* (25:22a). Holding up his glass of wine, Festus nodded, *"Tomorrow, you will hear him"* (25:22b).

~

The citizens of Caesarea did it up right. The palace hall, where the hearing was to be held, was adorned with extravagant decorations. We were welcomed by the music of stringed instruments and trumpets. Military officers and the city's most prominent people stood when Bernice and I entered. It was a welcome fit for a king...then again, I was their king! We were treated with all the splendor and honor due a Herod. This was a big deal; all the important people and officials were present.

So on the next day Agrippa and Bernice came with great pomp, and they entered the audience hall with the military tribunes and the prominent men of the city. (Acts 25:23a)

After everyone was seated the music stopped. *Then, at the command of Festus, Paul was brought in* (25:23b). At the sight of Paul, a low rumble of murmurings spread through the crowd. Flanked by guards on either side, with a chain around his waist, and hands bound, Paul slowly walked into the palace hall. To be honest, Paul wasn't what I expected. I expected a big, burly man, with an imposing demeanor. I expected a guy with a chip on his shoulder looking down with disdain upon his accusers. But that's not what Paul looked like. He was shorter than the average man, balding, and had a patchy, salt and pepper beard. Slightly bent over, he looked almost completely worn out for a man not yet sixty. He appeared to have trouble seeing clearly when he tried to focus on Festus. It was obvious this man had no easy life. However, the lines on his face spoke of determination and confidence. Leaving the chain around his waist, the guards untied his hands.

Because Paul appealed his case to Caesar, Festus had to officially charge Paul with some violation of Roman law.

A centurion called the proceeding to order, the crowd became silent. Fetus stood, and with the voice of an accomplished orator and with measured words, explained to those in attendance the reason for the hearing. He addressed the crowd, and drew their attention to the prisoner and the severity of the accusation. *"King Agrippa and all who are present with us, you see this man about whom the whole Jewish people petitioned me, both in Jerusalem and here, shouting that he ought not to live any longer"* (25:24).

Festus then gave his verdict, *"But I found that he had done nothing deserving death. And as he himself appealed to the emperor, I decided to go ahead and send him"* (25:25).

Again, the crowd began to murmur; the centurion ordered silence. Fetus continued, pleading for help in finding a charge against Paul, *"But I have nothing definite to write to my lord about him. Therefore I have brought him before you all, and especially before you, King Agrippa, so that, after we have examined him, I may have something to write. For it seems to me unreasonable, in sending a prisoner, not to indicate the charges against him"* (25:26-27).

When Festus was finished, I turned my attention to Paul. I could feel the eyes of everyone on me. Paul's gaze moved from Festus to me. It took him a moment to focus, but when he did, his dark, steel eyes seemed to pierce my very being. It took me by surprise. It made me uncomfortable. There was something different about this man. Even looking down from my high position, somehow Paul seem bigger, larger...*imposing*. Almost threatening. Not...not a physical threat, but something more. Something deeper. Something greater. Something chilling...to the soul. After an uncomfortable pause I said to Paul, *"You have permission to speak for yourself"* (26:1a).

After a moment of silently looking at me, as if sizing me up, he turned, commanding the attention of the audience. The small talk stopped. The palace hall fell completely silent. Then, with a dramatic motion of his hand, he began to speak with a voice that didn't match his body. He was loud, articulate, and confident. He directed his words to me, stretched out his hand and made his defense, *"I consider myself fortunate that it is before you, King Agrippa, I am going to make my defense today against all the accusations of the Jews, especially because you are familiar with all the customs and controversies of the Jews. Therefore I beg you to listen to me patiently"* (26:2-3).

What could I do? He had my full attention. I was captivated by this man Paul, and was compelled to listen. He continued, beginning with his personal story and establishing his credibility, *"My manner of life from my youth, spent from the beginning among my own nation and in Jerusalem, is known by all the Jews. They have known for a long time, if they are willing to testify, that according to the strictest party of our religion I have lived as a Pharisee"* (26:4-5). A Jew by birth and a Pharisee by profession, impressive credentials, I thought to myself. But, it was just like Festus said, this is a religious issue; it was a dispute between Jews and their religious beliefs.

Paul confirmed this by stating the charges against him, *"And now I stand here on trial because of my hope in the promise made by God to our fathers, to which our twelve tribes hope to attain, as they earnestly worship night and day. And for this hope I am accused by Jews, O king!"* (26:6-7). What is Paul talking about? What is the big issue? What is at the heart of the dispute? I was getting impatient. But then Paul got to the main issue, *"Why is it thought incredible by any of you that God raises the dead?"* (26:8).

That was the big issue? It was all about the resurrection of the dead. Whether or not Jesus was really raised from the dead? Then I realized, that is the game changer. If Jesus was still dead, there's no issue. Why the fuss? What threat is a dead man? What hope is there in someone who is in a grave? What can a dead man do? What power does a dead man have? But *if*...just *if*, Jesus *was* raised from the dead—what then? If Jesus is alive, he must be listened to. If Jesus is alive, his power must be respected. If Jesus is alive, we better give him an ear. If the God Paul preaches did raise Jesus from the dead, there must be life after death.

The thought of this possibility was disturbing. There's no way Jesus is alive. I wasn't there to witness his crucifixion, but I've seen plenty of Roman crucifixions in my life, and they're not pretty—neither are they survivable. Never has there been a report of a man crucified coming back to life—other than of course the reports about Jesus.

What Paul did next was masterful. He stated that at one time he too had the same convictions his accusers had. In fact, he was convinced he was doing the work of God by opposing Jesus' followers—these Christians. And not only that, the Jewish leaders themselves commissioned Paul's work against Christians. He went on, *"I myself was convinced that I ought to do many things in opposing the name of Jesus of Nazareth. And I did so in Jerusalem. I not only locked up many of the saints in prison after receiving authority from the chief priests, but when they were put to death I cast my vote against them. And I punished them often in all the synagogues and tried to make them blaspheme, and in raging fury against them I persecuted them even to foreign cities"* (26:9-11).

So, what changed Paul? Why after being raised a Jew—a devote Jew—did Paul change? Paul was an up-and-coming young Pharisee. He could be trusted to carry out, without question, the orders of the chief priest. Paul had it made; he was popular and respected; he had the best education; and he was on a career path that would take him right to the top. So, why the change of heart. Why throw it all away? What was it that drove Paul?

Paul answered that question for me when he recounted a life-changing experience he had while he was on his way to Damascus. Commissioned by the chief priests to arrest Christians in Damascus, Paul was blinded by a light from heaven that out-shone the noonday sun, *"In this connection I journeyed to Damascus with the authority and commission of the chief priests. At midday, O king, I saw on the way a light from heaven, brighter than the sun, that shone around me and those who journeyed with me"* (26:12-13).

Paul's demeanor changed while talking about his experience on the road to Damascus. He became deadly serious. As he spoke he occasionally closed his eyes as if experiencing it all again.

He went on. When the bright light appeared, he and those with him fell to the ground; Paul heard a voice from the heavens speaking to him, calling him by name. *"And when we had all fallen to the ground, I heard a voice saying to me in the Hebrew language, 'Saul, Saul, why are you persecuting me? It is hard for you to kick against the goads.'"* (26:14).

No doubt this was a supernatural event, but Paul was confused and wanted to know who was calling him from the heavens, accusing Paul of persecuting him. Paul got his answer, *"And I said, 'Who are you, Lord?' And the Lord said, 'I am Jesus whom you are persecuting"* (26:15). With that Paul paused, allowing me to take in what he just said.

Jesus? It was Jesus who was calling Paul? Paul claimed he was blinded by a light, brighter than the midday sun, and heard a voice calling him by name. That much I can believe; but Jesus? Jesus was dead. Dead men don't speak. Nevertheless, I allowed Paul to continue without interruption. He was an educated man. He was formerly with those who now wanted him dead. He seemed to have his senses about him, and this was something that he not only believed—he lived.

Paul didn't claim to be a Christian because it was popular, or safe, or provided an easy life. On the contrary, being a first century Christian wasn't popular and it promised a life of hardship—not ease. A life on the outside as more and more Christian-Jews were being excommunicated from their synagogues. Families disowned them, and those who ran business found themselves without customers. Employees found themselves without jobs. Rome still considered Christians to be part of the Jewish religion, and that provided them exemption from forced worship to Roman gods. But things were changing. If they were ban from worshipping in synagogues, Rome would be forced to look at Christians in a different light, and they would face persecution not only from Jewish authorities, but from Rome herself. And I believed that no religion would survive the wrath of the Roman government.

Paul, a Jewish Pharisee, claimed Jesus told him to be a witness for him and take a message to Gentiles, those who aren't Jews. Paul recounted Jesus' words, *"But rise and stand upon your feet, for I have appeared to you for this purpose, to appoint you as a servant and witness to the things in which you have seen me and to those in which I will appear to you, delivering you from your people and from the Gentiles—to whom I am sending you..."* (26:16-17).

My mind raced, I leaned forward, Paul's message included me. Although a Jew by religion, I really wasn't a Jew. I was a Gentile, what was the message? What was this all-important, life-changing message that Jesus told him to deliver? Paul continued, *"...to open their eyes, so that they may turn from darkness to light and from the power of Satan to God, that they may receive forgiveness of sins and a place among those who are sanctified by faith in me"* (26:18).

"That they may receive forgiveness of sins...by faith in me." Forgiveness of sins? *Receive*, forgiveness of sins by faith? That's the heart of the issue. I recalled the stories about how Jesus was condemned by the religious leaders after claiming he could forgive sin. The Jewish leaders rightly objected, they knew only God can forgive

sin. But, if Jesus really was raised from the dead, could he be God? This seems to be what Paul was asserting. And if Jesus *is* God and offers forgiveness of sin freely, that would strip religious leaders of power because access to heaven wouldn't be by appeasing them and obeying their silly rules. Is that why the religious leaders so vehemently objected? Was this whole thing an attempt by the religious leaders hold on to their power?

If, Jesus was not raised from the dead, then why all the concern? A dead man is powerless, just like other religious leaders that have come and gone from every religion under the sun. Even godly prophets of the Jews were never said to have the power to forgive sin. Take Abraham, Moses, Samuel, and Daniel. All godly men, some even performed miracles, but all died, and their bodies remain in their graves. Each of these revered men were righteous men, good and godly men, but none ever claimed to forgive sin, only Jesus. If Jesus was raised from the dead...?

Paul continued. He must have sensed I was in deep thought; again, he called me by name forcing me to stay focused on what he was saying. In case I missed it, Paul repeated the part about Jesus being raised from the dead. Knowing he had my attention, he caught a second wind. Although speaking to me, he addressed everyone with a powerful voice, *"Therefore, O King Agrippa, I was not disobedient to the heavenly vision, but declared first to those in Damascus, then in Jerusalem and throughout all the region of Judea, and also to the Gentiles, that they should repent and turn to God, performing deeds in keeping with their repentance. For this reason the Jews seized me in the temple and tried to kill me. To this day I have had the help that comes from God, and so I stand here testifying both to small and great, saying nothing but what the prophets and Moses said would come to pass: that the Christ must suffer and that, by being the first to rise from the dead, he would proclaim light both to our people and to the Gentiles"* (26:19-23).

Listening and calculating, Festus believed he got what he was looking for, something to write to Caesar explaining why Paul was on trial. Festus whispered to me that he planned to claim Paul is out of his mind. Paul's claim about seeing bright lights, hearing voices from the sky, and Jesus being alive—only an insane man would come up with such foolishness. Believing he had all he needed Festus interrupted Paul to gain support for his position. He stood, and with a loud voice said, *"Paul, you are out of your mind; your great learning is driving you out of your mind"* (26:24).

Festus tried to convince me to go along with him and he used this public forum to try and sway me. But I was raised in politics and saw right away what he was doing. Nevertheless, I was curious what Paul's response would be to Festus' accusation, so I said nothing. Paul responded directly and respectfully, *"I am not out of my mind, most excellent Festus, but I am speaking true and rational words"* (26:25).

Paul continued, once again personally appealing to me and the fact that everything about Jesus was open to public record, *"For the king knows about these things, and to him I speak boldly. For I am persuaded that none of these things has escaped his notice, for this has not been done in a corner"* (26:26).

Paul was right. Thirty years later, the death of Jesus was talked about like it happened yesterday. Furthermore, the claims of his resurrection by his followers were just as popular and no one could successfully dispute their claims. All one had to do is produce the body of Jesus, and no one had. The popular theory is that the body was stolen by his disciples while the Roman guards slept. But anyone that knows anything about Roman guards knows that's not true. If it were, the guards would have faced trial and severe punishment, even death, for falling asleep while on duty. There was never a formal military investigation. Perhaps Pilate never wanted to know the truth?

As Paul's testimony was coming to an end he questioned me. Talk about bold! An accused defending himself before a Roman court doesn't ask the court questions, but that's what Paul did. Paul addressed me directly and asked me a very pointed question, *"King Agrippa, do you believe the prophets? I know that you believe"* (26:27).

There was an uncomfortable silence as Paul's question hung in the air, *"Do you believe...I know that you believe."* While the courtroom was full of people, at that moment, I felt it was only Paul and me. His eyes fixed on mine, not wavering, not blinking, waiting for me to respond. He asked me a direct question, "Do I believe?" What he was asking is, *"Do I believe Jesus rose from the dead? Do I believe he will forgive my sin? Do I believe?"*

Paul called me to a decision—a public decision about Jesus. But it wasn't that simple. What would I do about this man called Jesus Christ? What are the implications if I embrace Jesus? What would others think? What would become of my position, could I retain it and declare I'm a Christian? What are the costs?

Bernice nudged me with her elbow, breaking my stare from Paul. It was then I realized the whole audience was still awaiting my response. I looked at all the people and suddenly felt the pressure of their opinion. What would they think of me? I offered my response, *"In a short time would you persuade me to be a Christian?"* (26:28). I was almost persuaded. But I wasn't ready. Paul made a good argument and I knew what he was saying was true, but I wasn't ready to give up all that I had.

There was disappointment in Paul's eyes. But he responded with genuine compassion and concern. Not only for me, but for everyone in attendance that day, *"Whether short or long, I would to God that not only you but also all who hear me this day might become such as I am—except for these chains"* (26:29).

With that Paul was finished, his hands were again bound, and he was led out by the guards. As Paul was led out there was a sadness felt throughout the audience. Paul's defense hit a cord with everyone. It made us all think. Paul's boldness and his willingness to give up everything, even his own liberty, to preach Jesus spoke to all.

Again, the eyes of everyone turned to me. They were waiting for me to say something more; but, for the first time that I could recall, I was at a loss for words. What more was there to be said? I just got up and left, Bernice and Festus followed me out.

Then the king rose, and the governor and Bernice and those who were sitting with them. (Acts 26:30)

When we had some privacy, Festus, Bernice, and I discussed Paul's case. We all agreed, the Jews had no case against Paul. Bernice summed up what we were thinking, *"This man is doing nothing to deserve death or imprisonment"* (26:31).

Why did Paul appeal to Caesar? Did he know what he was doing? Paul was an intelligent man; he knew the Jews had no case. I wish he'd just have allowed me to judge his case. I sighed deeply, looked at Festus and said, *"This man could have been set free if he had not appealed to Caesar"* (26:32).

~

King Agrippa lived to the age of 73.[4] There's no record of him ever becoming a Christian. The dispute between the religious leaders of Paul's day and today remains the focal point of Christianity—the resurrection of Jesus Christ from the dead.

Paul's question to King Agrippa was, "Do you believe?" Agrippa understood what Paul was asking him. It's the same questions Paul asks us, "Do you believe Jesus rose from the dead? Do you believe he will forgive your sin? Will you put your faith in Jesus?"

Through the evidence Paul presented he tried to persuade Agrippa to become a Christian, to believe Jesus died for his sins and rose from the dead. Paul wanted Agrippa to put his faith in Jesus for salvation. Not in religion, not in good works, not in a church, or in some priest, prophet, or pastor. But faith in a *person* —Jesus Christ.

7

OUTNUMBERED

I'd like to tell you my story. You call it a "testimony." It's a story of how God worked in my life. This is not my whole story but two significant incidents that changed my whole perspective on life. They were like those "ah ha" moments that tend to enlighten us to reality. These two events brought me to better understand the world and God working in it.

My name is Mispar, although my name is not mentioned in scripture. My name is not what's important, it's my story and what I learned. I lived in the Northern Kingdom of Israel during the ninth century, BC; my story is told in the book of Second Kings. Our understanding of God from scripture, and how he worked, was limited. At the time, only about half the Old Testament was available. It included: the first ten books of your English translations, which is Genesis through Second Samuel; Job; the writings and poetry of King David and King Solomon; and a few of the minor prophets. You must understand that we had an incomplete Old Testament because it was still being written. And, of course, it was over eight centuries before the New Testament.

The first event took place while I was attending school for

those wanting to follow God's call into the ministry. It was somewhat like today's seminaries that prepare pastors and missionaries for ministry. We studied and learned the scriptures available to us at the time. We were aspiring to be numbered among the men that became known as the *Sons of the Prophets*. Some of your Bibles call them the *Company of Prophets* or the *Group of Prophets*. Being named among the Sons of the Prophets was a great honor.

A prophet is one who spoke on God's behalf. Prophets were called to speak what the Lord spoke—no more and no less. That's what a faithful prophet did anyway—like modern day pastors and evangelists are supposed to do. In my day, just as today, people needed to hear from the Lord. They didn't need a commentary on current issues, politics, or entertainment. They needed to hear from God. It was the prophet's responsibility to ensure people knew and understood what the Lord expected of them.

The Sons of the Prophets are mentioned by name in chapter two of Second Kings. The great prophet Elijah was about to depart and pass his mantle onto Elisha. The Sons of the Prophets were there to witness their crossing of the Jordan River. Here's how the event is recorded:

The two prophets were in Bethel and Elijah said to Elisha, *"Please stay here, for the Lord has sent me to Jericho."*

Elisha refused, *"As the Lord lives, and as you yourself live, I will not leave you."*

They both crossed, and entered Jericho. The Lord had revealed to the Sons of the Prophets that Elijah was going to be taken by the Lord that very day. In Jericho the they asked Elisha, *"Do you know that today the Lord will take away your master from over you?"* The Lord had also informed Elisha, he answered, *"Yes, I know it; keep quiet."*

> *Elijah said to him, "Elisha, please stay here, for the Lord has sent me to Jericho." But he said, "As the Lord lives, and as you yourself live, I will not leave you." So they came to Jericho. The sons of the prophets who were at Jericho drew near to Elisha and said to him, "Do you know that today the Lord will take away your master from over you?" And he answered, "Yes, I know it; keep quiet." (2 Kings 2:4-5)*

I wasn't present to see that event; it was some years before I started school. However, that was the event that the Lord used to call me into the ministry.

Elijah, as great as he was, had his shortcomings. One was that he tended to go it alone. Perhaps you're familiar with the story of his depression when Jezebel threatened to kill him. He fled some two hundred miles south to Mt. Horeb and he cried out to God, *"I only, am left."* The Lord corrected Elijah, and told him there were some seven thousand that hadn't bowed the knee to a false god, I would later be one of the seven thousand.

Although Elijah was Elisha's mentor, Elisha was different; he had a better understanding of how God works in a community of people. Elisha understood the Lord had many others willing to follow him and do his work. Under the leadership of Elisha, the Sons of the Prophets grew in number. There were many of us willing to endure the rigors of school and face contempt, scorn, and even jail—or worse—from the government for speaking God's Word. In fact, in my first year of school there were so many of us the dormitory became overcrowded and needed to be expanded. The overcrowded dormitory led to my first eye-opening experience.

It was great to sit under the teaching of Elisha. He kept our attention and explained the Old Testament law to us in a way that made sense. Using practical illustrations, he explained how all the items in the temple had special significance, and helped to provide a deeper understanding of God. He also explained the Psalms and the difficult writings of Solomon to us.

But the crowded conditions were becoming unbearable, and I was voted spokesman for the group. That meant I had to approach Elisha with our grievances about the cramped conditions. I made an appointment and was called into the "Big House" to voice our complaint. Nervously, I shared with Elisha our concerns, *"The place where we dwell under your charge is too small for us."* I paused for his reaction.

"Yes, go on, Mispar," Elisha encouraged.

I continued, "We were thinking...hoping...wondering, if we can go down to the Jordan River, cut some logs and make a new dormitory for us to live in."

I waited for his response. He thought for a moment and then gave his blessing to build another facility with a simple one-word answer, *"Go."*

"Thank you, sir," I said, breathing a sigh of relief.

I hurried back and told the others the good news. Although I enjoyed the classroom instruction, I was excited to take a break from lectures and bookwork and get out in the fresh air. Besides, I was eager to show off my skill with an axe. Little did I know that I would learn more about God in one afternoon than I'd learned in a whole semester of school.

Before we headed out, one of the students begged Elisha to go with us, *"Be pleased to go with your servants."*

He agreed to tag along, *"I will go."*

Back then, most Israelites were farmers or shepherds; but my family worked construction. We were builders. My father tells me that my great-great-grandfather helped fell the huge cedar and cypress trees used to build Solomon's temple! I couldn't wait to show those farm-boys and sheep-herders how to fell a tree. It'd also be cool to show-off in front of my professor.

Now the sons of the prophets said to Elisha, "See, the place where we dwell under your charge is too small for us. Let us go to the Jordan and each of us get there a log, and let us make a place for us to dwell there." And he answered, "Go." Then one of them said, "Be pleased to go with your servants." And he answered, "I will go." (2 Kings 6:1-3)

Of course, we didn't have anything that cut trees, so we borrowed axes and saws from local folks that supported the school. Arriving at the river we got right to work. All through the morning things were going well. I was eagerly handing out instructions and showing the others how to use an axe and saw. Just before noon, I was explaining the proper swing of an axe to one student when things went bad.

"Stand back, let me give it a swing," I said to the greenhorn who was having trouble chopping through a stubborn tree.

Removing my cloak, I gave a couple practice swings then, with all the power I could muster, I lifted the axe above my head. I was just bringing it to bear when it suddenly lightened. Panic struck as I felt the axe head fly off behind me. I closed my eyes and waited for the iron to strike its mark. Splash! It landed harmlessly in the river! No one was hurt—just my pride. Then I remembered, it was borrowed!

I screamed for Elisha's help, *"Alas, my master! It was borrowed."* I spun around and ran to the riverbank in time to see the last ripples where the axe head had disappeared into the deep murky waters of the Jordan.

So he went with them. And when they came to the Jordan, they cut down trees. But as one was felling a log, his axe head fell into the water, and he cried out, "Alas, my master! It was borrowed." (2 Kings 6:4-5)

Elisha was relaxing under a group of palm trees carving a staff out of an oak branch when my hysterical outburst startled him. Responding to my desperate plea, Elisha calmly walked over to the bank where I stood staring hopelessly into the river. Seeing my distress, he put his hand on my shoulder and asked, "Mispar, *where did it fall?"* I pointed to the place. Elisha considered the waters.

Everyone stopped what they were doing and locked their attention on Elisha. After a moment, he grabbed a branch of a Joshua tree, cut off a piece, and threw it into the river. We were all staring at the stick drifting atop the water when up popped the axe head floating like it was a piece of wood! I looked at Elisha. He smiled and pointed to the axe head *"Take it up,"* he said.

The iron drifted to the edge of the bank. I reached down and picked it off the top of the water. It was that simple. *"Take it up,"* and all was well.

Then the man of God said, "Where did it fall?" When he showed him the place, he cut off a stick and threw it in there and made the iron float. And he said, "Take it up." So he reached out his hand and took it.(2 Kings 6:6-7)

At the time, losing the axe head seemed like a disaster. However, looking back with the wisdom that time and experience bring, losing an axe head wasn't all that big of a deal. No, it wasn't cheap, but it could be replaced. Likely, the gentleman that loaned it to us would've forgiven the debt. But that's not the point. The point is God is concerned about us. Like a mother who comforts her three-year-old with a skinned knee. Or, like a father that encourages his twelve-year-old that doesn't make the team. Like a grandfather that hugs his granddaughter who isn't asked to the dance—God is concerned about life's small trials.

The incident took place when I was a new believer. My faith was weak, and I needed to learn God loved me so much he would defy the laws of nature that he set in motion to retrieve a piece of iron—for *me*. I misunderstood the true nature of God. Somehow, I got the idea that God was an angry, impersonal, faraway deity that needed to be appeased by hard work.

Knowing the Lord controls nature, you'd think I understood he controls nations. I guess I wasn't the sharpest arrow in the quiver. This brings me to the next incident.

Sometime after I finished up my formal schooling I was privileged to work directly under Elisha. We were living in Dothan. Dothan was a small city not far from Israel's northern border and about eleven miles north of the capital city, Samaria. I was a servant in Elisha's house. "Servant" might not sound like a glorious title but think about servants in the Bible. Servants are those who serve others. Joseph served Pharaoh. Joshua served Moses. Long before David became king he served Saul. Both Moses and Job were called servants of God. So, I figured I was in good company. I think I was right, since later, you would get to read Jesus' own words telling others that he *came not to be served but to serve.*

For even the Son of Man came not to be served but to serve, and to give his life as a ransom for many. (Mark 10:45)

It was an unstable time for Israel. After Solomon's reign, the kingdom split and remained so until after the Babylonian exile some four-hundred years later. While the Southern Kingdom of Judah enjoyed a number godly kings, those of us in the Northern Kingdom didn't have even one. The result was God's constant—yet loving—discipline in the form of foreign nations threatening and attacking us. You think we'd have learned. But we didn't, and the people of Israel lived in constant fear of attack by superior forces. During my day, the nation of Syria, on our northern border, posed an ever-increasing threat.

The Syrian king, Ben-Hadad II, launched a series of raids into northern Israel. He was hoping to catch Israel's army flatfooted and defeat it in one swift, surprise attack. King Ben-Hadad secretly instructed his officers where to set up camp to ambush Israel's army in surprise attacks. *"At such and such a place shall be my camp,"* he advised his officers.

Once when the king of Syria was warring against Israel, he took counsel with his servants, saying, "At such and such a place shall be my camp." (2 Kgs. 6:8)

God revealed to Elisha Ben-Hadad's plans and Elisha routinely sent me to Joram, Israel's king, warning him about Syria's plans. In counter-moves, King Joram relocated his army to a position of advantage and to avoid an ambush. Over time, I delivered a number of these dispatches.

Needless to say, King Joram appreciated the information. On the other hand, King Ben-Hadad became frustrated with Israel's counter-intelligence. He wondered how in the world Israel was getting this top-secret information. Unable to figure it out, he became suspicious—some would say even a bit paranoid. He suspected a double-agent among his highest ranking and most trusted officers. Frustrated he couldn't figure out who was responsible, he ordered an investigation.

But the man of God sent word to the king of Israel, "Beware that you do not pass this place, for the Syrians are going down there." And the king of Israel sent to the place about which the man of God told him. Thus he used to warn him, so that he saved himself there more than once or twice. (2 Kgs. 6:9-10)

I can picture King Ben-Hadad yelling at his aide, "Send me my intelligence officer, I'm going to get to the bottom of this! I want to know who is sharing top secret information with Israel." Syria's intelligence division launched an intense investigation to flush out the mole. No one was beyond suspicion. Each officer was interviewed and investigated then re-interviewed. No stone was left unturned. Finally, there was a break in the case. The findings were presented to the king. *"Elisha, the prophet who is in Israel, tells the king of Israel the words that you speak in your bedroom."*

> *And the mind of the king of Syria was greatly troubled because of*
> *this thing, and he called his servants and said to them, "Will you*
> *not show me who of us is for the king of Israel?" And one of his*
> *servants said, "None, my lord, O king; but Elisha, the prophet*
> *who is in Israel, tells the king of Israel the words that you speak*
> *in your bedroom." (2 Kgs. 6:11-12)*

Ben-Hadad was enraged. A civilian—*a religious leader of all people*—was accessing top secret information! Ben-Hadad demanded to know the whereabouts of Elisha and ordered his immediate capture, *"Go and see where he is, that I may send and seize him."* It was no secret where Elisha lived, and it was reported to the Syrian king, *"Behold, he is in Dothan."* King Ben-Hadad wasted no time. That very night he surrounded the city with a contingent of horses, chariots, and a large army.

> *And he said, "Go and see where he is, that I may send and seize*
> *him." It was told him, "Behold, he is in Dothan." So he sent there*
> *horses and chariots and a great army, and they came by night*
> *and surrounded the city. (2 Kgs. 6:13-14)*

As usual, I was the first one up that morning. I opened the shudders allowing the fresh, brisk, morning air to cool the house before the day's heat set in. Then I grabbed a couple water buckets and headed out to the well to draw water. I was half way across the courtyard when I noticed light flickering in the foothills. Stopping to take a closer look, I realized it was the early morning sun reflecting off swords, shields, spears, and chariots. Then I saw a flag—the Syrian army! I looked around and saw that the city was completely surrounded. I dropped the water buckets and ran back into the house. Elisha walked into the dining room, yawned a "Good morning," oblivious that we were surrounded by the enemy. I told him the dilemma we were in and asked him what we were going to do. This was no lost axe head that fell into the water—this was the powerful Syrian army, and we were surrounded! This was a life and death situation. Why didn't Elisha see this coming? But to look at Elisha, you'd think it was simply another piece of iron in the river. I stared hopelessly at Elisha. Seeing my distress, he put his hand on my shoulder, gave me a reassuring grin and said, "Mispar, *do not be afraid, for those who are with us are more than those who are with them.*"

When the servant of the man of God rose early in the morning and went out, behold, an army with horses and chariots was all around the city. And the servant said, "Alas, my master! What shall we do?" He said, "Do not be afraid, for those who are with us are more than those who are with them." (2 Kgs. 6:15-16)

I took my eyes off Elisha and looked around the house. There was no one with us—no one that would do any good. There was the cook, whose quarters were attached to the kitchen, and in the bunkhouse, there were about thirty other prophets. I figured we had thirty-three men, thirty-five tops, but—there was an army outside. Besides, what were we to arm ourselves with? Scrolls and inkwells?

My worried eyes went back to Elisha. He smiled and closed his eyes and prayed aloud, *"O Lord, please open his eyes that he may see."* Again, I looked around the house, nothing—just Elisha and me, but Elisha pointed to a window. I walked to it and looked out at the mountains. I could hardly believe my eyes. Beyond the foothills was an army much more imposing than the Syrian army. This was an army of huge, powerful beings astride horses and chariots that had wheels with fire leaping from them. The horses reared on their hind legs and snorted fire. I shuttered at the sight of the magnificent display of force. This was heaven's army. Truly, we had a superior force.

Then Elisha prayed and said, "O Lord, please open his eyes that he may see." So the Lord opened the eyes of the young man, and he saw, and behold, the mountain was full of horses and chariots of fire all around Elisha. (2 Kgs. 6:17)

Unaware of heaven's army breathing down their necks, the Syrians marched down from the mountains and right up to our farm. Elisha stood on the front porch like he was expecting a visit from an old friend. The officer in charge, along with four chariots, drove into our front yard, trampling the freshly planted garden and sending the goats scurrying. The officer dismounted with a look of disdain on his face. He looked around as if to say, "Is this the place?" Convinced he had the right place, he started toward us with several junior officers at his heels. Elisha countered with a smile on his face and motioned him to come. With his hand still raised, Elisha closed his eyes and prayed, *"Please strike this people with blindness."* The officer stopped and looked around as if confused. The other soldiers did the same. Elisha bid them come closer. Hesitant, the officer and his men approached and, with a genuine smile, Elisha offered his assistance, *"This is not the way, and this is not the city. Follow me, and I will bring you to the man whom you seek."*

Elisha had me fetch and saddle the horses. I led the horses from the barn to Elisha. We mounted up and I looked to the mountains, but the heavenly army was gone! I gave Elisha a nervous look. He looked to the mountains and back at me then, smiled and winked; "Samaria," he said.

And when the Syrians came down against him, Elisha prayed to the Lord and said, "Please strike this people with blindness." So he struck them with blindness in accordance with the prayer of Elisha. 19 And Elisha said to them, "This is not the way, and this is not the city. Follow me, and I will bring you to the man whom you seek." And he led them to Samaria. (2 Kgs. 6:18-19)

A couple hours later, we were nearing Samaria with a clueless Syrian army in tow. As soon as Samaria's watchman reported the Syrian army approaching protocol demanded that the city gates be closed and locked, and Israel's soldiers ordered to their battle stations to prepare for combat. Knowing this, Elisha sent me ahead to inform King Joram of the plan. The king was shocked and didn't know what to do,

"So, what do we do, just let them walk into our city?" King Joram asked.

"That's what Elisha wants," I said.

The king was clearly worried, "Open the city gates to an enemy army? That doesn't make sense," he said, more to himself than me. The king continued, anxiously pacing, and talking to himself. "But then little that Elisha does makes sense. Did Elisha switch sides? Was this some kind of trap?" he mumbled.

Then he looked back at me, "Let me seek counsel."

I was ushered outside the room while King Joram consulted with his advisors. A few minutes later, I was asked back inside.

The king addressed me, "Okay, I'll go along. But I'm putting the army on high alert. I'm canceling all leave and recalling every man. Soldiers will be stationed around the wall when they get here. The archers will stand at the ready."

I was dismissed and rode out to rejoin Elisha, now half a mile outside Samaria. Elisha didn't ask what was said, he simply nodded acknowledging my return. We rode in silence through the open gate, right into the middle of town.

People waved to Elisha, and he waved back. We reigned to a stop and I heard the gates close behind us. Elisha broke his silence with a prayer, *"O Lord, open the eyes of these men, that they may see."*

The Syrian army let out a collective gasp when they realized they were in the middle of Samaria, surrounded by Israel's army. Just as King Joram said, he had his soldiers ready. When Elisha stopped the parade of Syrian soldiers they found themselves surrounded by the Israelite army with their bows at full draw.

> *As soon as they entered Samaria, Elisha said, "O Lord, open the eyes of these men, that they may see." So the Lord opened their eyes and they saw, and behold, they were in the midst of Samaria. (2 Kgs. 6:20)*

Excited, King Joram was ready to finish them off there and then. He raised his right hand and prepared to drop it signaling for the archers to let their arrows fly. Like a giddy little child, he asked Elisha permission to shoot, *"My father, shall I strike them down? Shall I strike them down?"*

The Syrian officer and his soldiers were understandably terrified. Confused, they looked around and started to comprehend their dire situation. Somehow, they ended up in the middle of their enemy's capital city, entirely surrounded by an army with drawn bows. *Ambushed with no escape!* The very thing they had been trying to do to Israel, but now the tables were turned.

> As soon as the king of Israel saw them, he said to Elisha, "My father, shall I strike them down? Shall I strike them down?" He answered, "You shall not strike them down. Would you strike down those whom you have taken captive with your sword and with your bow? Set bread and water before them, that they may eat and drink and go to their master."(2 Kgs. 6:21-22)

Nervous, I started to consider my own situation. Elisha and I were right in the middle of it—literally between the two armies! "I hope those archers are good shots," I thought to myself. I looked around—no heavenly army in sight. The crowd had grown larger and started shouting, echoing the king's words, "Strike them down! Strike them down!" I was waiting for Elisha to give the okay for the king to lower his hand, but he didn't. Elisha raised his arms and motioned for quiet. When the crowd quieted down, he addressed King Joram, *"You shall not strike them down. Would you strike down those whom you have taken captive with your sword and with your bow? Set bread and water before them, that they may eat and drink and go to their master."*

Feed them and let them go? Why would Elisha want that? We had them dead to rights. They invaded our country with the intention of seizing one of our citizens and charging him with spying. Syria was the aggressor. Israel had every right to defend herself, but that's not what Elisha commanded. He wanted us to feed them and send them back home, so that's what King Joram did.

That was one big bar-b-que! The king declared a holiday and the whole city enjoyed a great dinner as we dined with our enemy. After they ate their full, they returned to King Ben-Hadad fat and happy. You know, that put an end to Syria's raids. At least for some time.

So he prepared for them a great feast, and when they had eaten and drunk, he sent them away, and they went to their master. And the Syrians did not come again on raids into the land of Israel. (2 Kgs. 6:23)

It was a wake-up call for both nations. Israel was reminded to trust the Lord; he is their Savior and Protector. It was a great lesson for God's people. Israel learned the Lord is in control and Syria only has power because the Lord God Almighty allows it. Syria learned that there is a God in Israel that is more powerful than the army or the gods of Syria.

～

These two incidents taught me more about God than years of schooling could have. First, in the axe head incident, I learned that God is love. This was no longer a cliché, it was real for me. When I realized God was concerned about an old iron axe head I borrowed, I understood how deep his love is for me. Years later, in the New Testament, Jesus expressed the lesson I learned, *"Are not two sparrows sold for a penny? And not one of them will fall to the ground apart from your Father. But even the hairs of your head are all numbered"* (Matt. 10:29-30).

The incident changed my prayer life, and I started taking everything to the Lord in prayer. Before learning that lesson, I tried to handle life's little problems. But after it, I started giving everything over to the Lord. No, that doesn't mean I went through life trouble free! Far from it. In fact, through the years of my life I experienced my share, maybe even more than my share, of troubles. I prayed to the Lord and he answered my prayers. More often than not, the answer wasn't what I wanted, but looking back, it's what I needed.

Life's little trials toughen us up for life's bigger trials. The Lord doesn't exempt us from this world's problems, but he's there to walk through the trials with us. Name one character in the Bible that didn't face adversity. You can't. And the one that faced the most was the very Son of God, Jesus Christ.

The second incident, the Syrian army incident, taught me that God is sovereign, and he's in control. When my eyes were opened, and I saw the host of heaven's army, all fear left. The sight of them reassured me that the Lord has things well in hand even when it doesn't look like it. That morning, all my fear was taken away. Did that mean I never feared again? I wish I could say that was the case, but even after that experience things in life still frightened me. Fear drove me to pray for strength and a deeper faith. When I prayed, the Lord brought that incident to mind and my fears departed, just as the Syrian army departed Samaria that day.

The lesson learned was not to fear man, but to fear the Lord. Jesus also summed up this lesson. He put it this way, *"And do not fear those who kill the body but cannot kill the soul. Rather fear him who can destroy both soul and body in hell"* (Matt. 10:28).

8

THE INN CROWD

I'd like to tell you a story; it's my story. You call it a "testimony." It's a story of how God worked in my life. I was an ancient small-town business owner, and anyone who's tried to keep a family business profitable in a small-town understands the struggle.

According to your calendar, I was born in an era that's referred to today as BC, meaning "Before Christ." It's the calendar commissioned by Pope Gregory XIII in 1582. This calendar uses the birth of Jesus Christ as the turning point in history to universally reckon time. Today, it's the most widely used international calendar. You live in the twenty-first century AD. "AD" is short for the Latin term "An-no Dom-i-ni" which translates to "The year of our Lord." I was born BC, Before Christ.

The town I lived in was about six miles south of Jerusalem. Perhaps you've heard of it? It's called Bethlehem. Jerusalem was the big city—it was the happening place; and much of my business depended on what was happening in Jerusalem. In my day, Bethlehem was just a small village on the outskirts of Jerusalem. It was too far away for people living in Bethlehem to commute daily to Jerusalem. But it was close enough for travelers to stay when there was no lodging available in the big city.

Each year, I depended on three Jewish feasts that brought people to Jerusalem. They were the springtime feast called Passover, the early summer wheat-harvest feast known as Pentecost, and a fall fruit-harvest feast named the Feast of Booths. My business depended heavily on these three annual pilgrimages to Jerusalem. See, I ran a small hotel in Bethlehem, named *The Inn*. Locally, I was known simply as the Innkeeper.

Although generally regarded as an insignificantly small town, long before my time, Bethlehem was an important city. It's mentioned many times in the Old Testament scriptures. Jacob's wife Rachel, the mother of Joseph and Benjamin, was buried in Bethlehem. It's where Ruth met Boaz, and of course it was the birthplace and hometown of Ruth's great-grandson, David, who became Israel's greatest king. But most important it was the focal point of the great promise given by the prophet Micah. Micah said the *one who is to be ruler* will be born in Bethlehem.

But you, O Bethlehem Ephrathah, who are too little to be among the clans of Judah, from you shall come forth for me one who is to be ruler in Israel, whose coming forth is from of old, from ancient days.(Micah 5:2)

This was the promise that the Messiah, the Christ, the Anointed One would be born in our little town! Oh, how we Jews looked forward to the coming of our King to relieve us from Roman oppression. But it had been over 700 years since Micah wrote those words and to tell you the truth most people in our little town had forgotten the promise, or didn't really believe it. Sure, there was still the hope that God would get us out from under Roman rule, but to be frank, we'd become used to it.

In fact, many of us were comfortable with it. Rome wasn't all bad. They let us worship as we pleased as long as we kept to ourselves and didn't try to convert any Romans to Judaism. We were free to work and make a living; and Rome did offer protection from attack. It may have been a pagan and immoral society, but most Jews got along just fine. Nevertheless, somewhere, deep down inside each Jew was a hope that the Christ would come and make things right.

That was the state of affairs when I lived in Bethlehem and ran *The Inn.* Like King David, I came from a family of shepherds. My father and both my grandfathers were shepherds. My brothers followed suit. In fact, my younger brother's flock was in the field, a couple miles out of town when my story takes place. He and his men were camped out watching over the flock that night. I shepherded for a time, but thought I'd try my hand in the hospitality business. I sold my flock and purchased a small building that I converted into several rooms to rent out to guests.

As I said earlier, keeping a small-town family business profitable can be difficult. We relied heavily on the overflow of Jerusalem's inns during the three big feasts. But I also needed the tourists that came from time to time to visit the burial place of Rachel or see David's ancestral home. And during the sheering season we always had an influx of guests—mostly workers who could afford to pay for a room. It provided a decent living for the wife and me. Speaking of the wife, it was just her and me. We never had any children, but there were always a number of nieces and nephews around. But little did we know that our little inn, and the manger out back, would become one of the biggest tourist attractions the world has ever known.

My story is recorded in the Gospel of Luke, chapter two.

Every year after the fall Feast of Booths, the wife and I looked forward to the winter break. Normally there wasn't much travel during the winter, and things slowed down in Bethlehem. I often took the opportunity to repair things around the place and my wife worked to inventory and replenish our storeroom. One winter, I was just beginning my routine maintenance when we were overrun by people coming to Bethlehem. It was the biggest flood of people I'd ever seen in our little town. This is really where my story starts. It begins, *"In those days..."* when the Roman Emperor, Caesar Augustus, issued an order that everyone needed to be registered.

In those days a decree went out from Caesar Augustus that all the world should be registered.(Luke 2:1)

About twenty-five years earlier Octavian, known as Caesar Augustus, finally secured sole authority when he won a critical victory over Mark Antony. Since that time, Rome was really experiencing a period of peace. In fact, Augustus was known as the emperor of peace.[1] So, although Rome was an occupying force, things weren't really all that bad. However, there was still a strong debate amongst the Jewish people about the appropriate role of Rome and its government in our lives. The extremes were the Herodians, who sided with the Roman government and lined their pockets from government revenue. On the other side were the Zealots, who hated the Roman government and sought to overthrow it at every turn. But most Jews weren't so caught up in the politics. They were just focused on putting food on the table, making a comfortable living, and enjoying the athletic games and the beautiful countryside.

Now the time came for those living in Palestine to register. This registration order was for paying taxes, since the vast majority of the people living in Palestine were Jewish, the Jewish tradition to take a census was invoked. This required the head of all households to return to his birthplace for registration.

And all went to be registered, each to his own town.(Luke 2:3)

Being the typical small country town, most young people moved away from Bethlehem when they realized they needed to make money to survive. With its large families and limited means for earning a living, it was unusual for adult children to stay. Even knowing this, when the order to register went out, I never expected so many people to show up.

Our little inn quickly filled. In fact, we were double and even triple booking rooms. Every square foot of our lodging place was being used. For the first couple of days, people were considerate and friendly. But then things went downhill—fast. Apparently, the government didn't expect so many people either, and they were unprepared and disorganized. This resulted in people staying longer than planned; and with the cramped conditions, tensions mounted and nerves quickly began to wear thin with the inn crowd.

I was making good money, but I was beginning to wonder if it was worth it. The missus and I even rented out our own bedroom and were sleeping in the office area on a makeshift bed of straw and blankets. There was simply no more room in the inn. People were constantly complaining, and we were at our wits end. They grumbled about the cold outside and the heat inside. Food and feed prices had soared giving them something else to lament. Then people started discussing the issue of taxes and that really set things off. What began as enjoyable conversation and company turned into heated debates, quarrels, and politically-charged arguments.

Not only that, people were making a mess of the place. Leaving trash and uneaten food lying around and not cleaning up after their animals that were packed in the stables almost as tight as we were packed in the inn. It had been several days and there was no end in sight.

People were still knocking at the door looking for a place to stay. Couldn't they read, "No Vacancy"? Still they came knocking. At first, I was polite and gently told them no, we were full and had no room. But day after day (and night after night) brought me to the end of civility. Soon, I simply opened the door and yelled, "No!" before slamming it shut. "Just leave me alone," I thought. "Let me have a little peace!"

One evening as usual, right in the middle of supper, *knock, knock, knock!* I rolled my eyes in frustration and was relieved when my wife said she'd take care of it. "Thank you, dear. Just send them on their way," I sighed.

A few minutes later my wife returned, "Honey, will you please come outside?" "What? Why? What is the problem?" I thought. I tossed down my spoon, got up, and walked outside and found— you guessed it—travelers wanting a place to stay. Why couldn't she just tell them, "No!"?

It was a strong looking young man and his wife. "Honey, this is Joseph and Mary. They've come a long way and need a place to stay," my wife said.

Wonderful! She knows their names! Now I knew this was going to be an uphill battle. Then, to make matters worse, I saw the young lady named Mary was pregnant. And boy was she pregnant!

> *And Joseph also went up from Galilee, from the town of Nazareth, to Judea, to the city of David, which is called Bethlehem, because he was of the house and lineage of David, to be registered with Mary, his betrothed, who was with child.* (Luke 2:4-5)

My wife pleaded with me, "Can't we do something? They told me they are both related to King David."

I groaned, "Half the people in Bethlehem are related to King David. Do you know how many wives he had? Besides, you know we don't have any room. There's just no place at all."

The young man named Joseph spoke up, "But sir, we'll stay anywhere. Even out with the animals. I just need a place for my wife, she's due any day now."

"You're willing to stay with animals?"

"Yes, anywhere we can to get out of the weather and have a little privacy" he said.

"All right, the stables are out back. And I'll only charge you half price," I said.

My wife slapped me on the arm. "You'll do no such thing; they can stay for free. I'll not charge someone for sleeping with animals!"

Joseph looked relieved, "Thank you sir and ma'am, I am grateful for your kindness. I'll be more than happy to pay," he said.

"We'll not have it. Follow me," my wife said emphatically, and led the young couple around back. She looked back at me, "You too!"

I moved a pair of camels out of one of the stalls and went to gather some hay—hay that I could sell. Mary took a seat on a stool while Joseph unloaded their donkey. I returned with the hay and found my wife had raked the stall clean and brought a candle from the inn for them to use.

"Get more hay," she told me.

"More?" I questioned.

"Yes, more," she said. I thought to myself, "Not only am I not making money, I'm losing money."

"And bring a feeding trough that can be used as a crib," she added.

"This baby is quickly becoming an inconvenience in my life," I mumbled.

"What's that dear?" the wife asked.

"Nothing. Nothing at all," I said.

For the next several days, things continued to be hectic around the inn. We were told it would still take some time for the government to get everyone properly accounted for and registered. In the meantime, my wife constantly checked on the couple and, gave me unsolicited reports as to Mary's condition. "It'll be anytime now!" she said like the baby was somebody special, one of her own grandchildren or something.

One evening, I was extremely exhausted and turned in early. It had been a busy day, but things were beginning to settle down. It was that very night, a seemingly ordinary night, that while I slept my world changed. In fact, everyone's world changed. Not long after I drifted off to sleep, I was momentarily awakened from my slumber by a rap on the door. "Who's that?" I asked my wife.

"It's Joseph, he needs more cloths," she said.

"Okay, goodnight," and with that I went to sleep.

Looking back, I recall that it was unusually quiet that evening, actually peaceful I'd say. For some reason, the inn crowd were kinder to each other. The children remained cheerful while they played games of tag and hide-and-seek. The arguments turned back into civil conversation. Tension was replaced with laughter. A remarkable sense of harmony hung in the air of the crowded little inn as I again drifted off to sleep.

Of course, I can't tell you firsthand what happened while I slept, but I can tell you what was reported to me by my brother when later that night, I was awakened to the news that Mary delivered her son.

And while they were there, the time came for her to give birth. And she gave birth to her firstborn son and wrapped him in swaddling cloths and laid him in a manger, because there was no place for them in the inn. (Luke 2:6-7)

Remember, my brother was a shepherd, and he said it started out as any other night. Apparently, even the shepherds were experiencing difficulties with the over-crowding in Bethlehem. With all the people in town, they were forced to move their skittish flocks further out than normal for that time of year. Like the people in town, the shepherds had to compete for the best grazing areas, and were at each other's throats. Then to top things off, several days of wind and drizzling rain made for miserable outdoor living conditions. But that day, just before dusk, the skies cleared up and the winds became calm. He shared that the sunset was gorgeous and seemed to mesmerize the shepherds as they sat around an inviting and warming fire as the night air cooled.

And in the same region there were shepherds out in the field, keeping watch over their flock by night. (Luke 2:8)

My brother assigned the night-watches, and most of the men

turned in for what appeared to be a welcomed night of peaceful sleep. But suddenly they were awakened by a light so brilliant that it illuminated the night's sky and made my brother momentarily believe he slept past sunup. A huge figure stood before him. The being looked like a man, but this was no human. He stood two feet taller than any man my brother had ever seen and glowed with such brightness the shepherds had to shield their eyes.

And an angel of the Lord appeared to them, and the glory of the Lord shone around them, and they were filled with great fear. (Luke 2:9)

The shepherds stepped back, and unconsciously held their staffs at the ready to protect the sheep. But shaking in their sandals, they felt helpless and foolish. My brother was amazed to see the sheep were peacefully sleeping or grazing. Then he realized this could only be an angel of God!

The angel spoke slowly and methodically allowing his words to sink into the minds and hearts of the startled shepherds. The angel began telling them not to be afraid, he came with good news, *"Fear not, for behold, I bring you good news of great joy that will be for all the people."*

There was a collective sigh of relief as the shepherds lowered their staffs and listened. The angel continued, *"For unto you is born this day in the city of David a Savior, who is Christ the Lord."* Again, the angel paused.

"What did he say?" one of the shepherds said aloud, to no one in particular.

"The Christ is born," my brother answered.

"Who?" a young shepherd asked.

"The Christ, the Messiah. The one who will sit on David's

thrown," my brother said. The angel continued, *"And this will be a sign for you: you will find a baby wrapped in swaddling cloths and lying in a manger."*

And the angel said to them, "Fear not, for behold, I bring you good news of great joy that will be for all the people. For unto you is born this day in the city of David a Savior, who is Christ the Lord. And this will be a sign for you: you will find a baby wrapped in swaddling cloths and lying in a manger." (Luke 2:10-12)

At that moment, the sky burst open with thousands upon thousands of angels all giving glory to God in unison. They were saying, *"Glory to God in the highest, and on earth peace among those with whom he is pleased!"*

And suddenly there was with the angel a multitude of the heavenly host praising God and saying, "Glory to God in the highest, and on earth peace among those with whom he is pleased!" (Luke 2:13-14)

Just as suddenly as they appeared, they were gone. The brightness and loud praising were replaced by darkness and silence. The shepherds were dumbfounded. The sheep still seemed clueless, unmoved by what happened. Was it real? Did this really happen? My brother looked at the other men. Finally, one broke the silence suggesting they check out what the angel said, *"Let us go over to Bethlehem and see this thing that has happened, which the Lord has made known to us."*

When the angels went away from them into heaven, the shepherds said to one another, "Let us go over to Bethlehem and see this thing that has happened, which the Lord has made known to us." (Luke 2:15)

That made sense. That would confirm what they saw. "Who wants to stay with the sheep?" my brother asked. No hands went up. He wasn't sure if it was fear of the angels returning or missing out on seeing the Messiah.

"They'll be fine, we'll check and come right back," one of the men said.

"Okay, but let's make it quick, I don't want to leave the sheep unprotected for long," my brother said, and with that headed into town.

The shepherds started out walking and talking about what they'd seen. "How do we know where to look?" one asked.

"We'll start with the closest stable and work our way through town until we find the baby," my brother said.

The closer they got to town the quicker they went. Soon, all the shepherds were almost running with expectation. They arrived at the first two stables and found nothing but restless animals. Then they came to my stable.

My brother described the scene for me. As he entered the stable area he saw the dim light from the candle dancing off the back side of the stall where Joseph and Mary were. He heard Mary gently humming and he knew he'd found the place. Not wanting to intrude, my brother called out, "Hello?"

Joseph emerged, "Yes, what is it? Can I help you?"

"We were told the Christ is born," my brother said.

"Who told you?" Joseph questioned suspiciously.

"An angel," my brother replied.

Joseph shifted his weight and asked, "An angel? What did he look like?" My brother described what they saw and Joseph relaxed. He smiled, nodded, and invited them back. "Mary, we have visitors."

"And then I saw him." My brother's eyes misted over as he recalled the moment when he stepped inside the tiny stall. They laid him in a feeding trough of all places! He was asleep, tightly wrapped up in white cloths and snuggled in the warmth of the hay. A little baby boy sound asleep without a care in the world while, his mother softly hummed a lullaby. "May I touch him?" my brother asked Mary. She nodded her head and my brother gently touched the baby's forehead. He insists the baby smiled.

He thanked Joseph and Mary and told the other shepherds to quickly to look and then leave the family alone. One by one the shepherds filed past quietly staring at the little baby boy like it was the first infant they'd ever seen.

And they went with haste and found Mary and Joseph, and the baby lying in a manger. (Luke 2:16)

Knock! Knock! Knock! came the loud rap on my door awakening me from a deep sleep. My brother barged in and I was immediately fully awake, "What's wrong?"

"Nothing, brother, nothing at all. You know the couple staying in your stable?" he asked.

"Yes, yes, Joseph and Mary, why?"

"She had her baby," he said. With that my wife popped up and ran out.

"So, what's the point? Another baby, another mouth to feed, another head to be counted for Roman registration. What's the big deal?" I yawned. My heartrate was slowly going back to normal, and I was far more interested in getting a little bit more sleep than worrying about how my brother knew that Mary had her baby.

"Sit back down brother. Let me tell you about this child born in your stable." He recounted the story. The angels, Joseph, Mary, and the baby. I would have doubted it, if it wasn't coming from my brother. Still, I questioned him.

"Are you sure?" I asked. He was unusually excited. I'd never seen him so enthusiastic, even at the birth of his own children and grandchildren. But here he was, in the middle of the night, giving me news about a baby born in my stable. It made me wonder.

And when they saw it, they made known the saying that had been told them concerning this child. And all who heard it wondered at what the shepherds told them. (Luke 2:17-18)

I walked out into the cool of the night, and a chill went through my body. I wasn't sure if it was from the cool air or from my brother's report. I looked up to the heavens. The stars seemed brighter than usual. I walked back to the stable, and found my wife cuddling the baby in her arms with Mary and Joseph at her side.

When I passed by my wife, she handed me the baby. A bit surprised, I took the child in my arms and brought him to my chest. His dark eyes considered mine and a strange peace came over me.

"How are you, Mary?" I asked.

"I'm fine," she said confidently if not a little sleepy.

"And how's the father?" I asked Joseph.

Joseph started to say something, paused, and then smiled, "He's great, I'm sure." Was his perplexing answer.

"Thank you so much for your kindness," Mary said. "I'll treasure these memories in my heart.

Mary treasured up all these things, pondering them in her heart.
(Luke 2:19)

"Come now, dear," I said to my wife. "I'm sure Mary and the baby need their rest. Let's give the family a little privacy."

We returned to the office and talked to my brother who filled us in on all the details of what he and the other shepherds witnessed in the field. He recounted the appearance of the first angel and his words, then the sudden appearance of all the other angels and their glorifying God, and lastly their message that peace has come to earth.

"We need to get back to our flocks, brother," and with that, he and the other shepherds headed back to the fields praising God for all they had heard and seen.

And the shepherds returned, glorifying and praising God for all they had heard and seen, as it had been told them. (Luke 2:19)

It was now after four in the morning. Neither the wife nor I could go back to sleep. She warmed up some hot cider, and we sat quietly considering the things we heard and wondering about what my brother had told us. What does this mean? Is this baby boy that's sleeping out in the stables the promised Messiah? Is he the one? Will he bring peace to this broken world? Will he be the Savior of Israel? But the *"good news"* was *"for all...people"* if I recall my brother's words correctly.

Then I recalled again a prophecy from Micah, *"And he shall be their peace."*

I almost missed it. If my brother hadn't come and shared the good news, I would have missed the first Christmas.

$$\sim$$

"Christmas" is the term used today to celebrate Christ's birth. Christmas is a combination of two words, "Christ's Mass." Mass comes from a Latin word that came to mean "mission." Hence, Christmas is "Christ's Mission."

Jesus is the promised Christ, the Messiah, the Anointed One. But he didn't come as many Jews expected to relieve Israel from Roman oppression. He came as the promised Redeemer of humanity to relieve us from sin's punishment and to offer God's forgiveness. Christ's mission was to redeem humanity back to the Father by his sacrificial death on the cross. He succeeded in his mission. Have you accepted your Christmas gift from God? Don't you miss out on Christ's mission.

9

PRAGMATIC BELIEF

I'd like to tell you my story. You call it a "testimony." It's a story of how God worked in my life, and you can read it in what you call the New Testament. You see, when I was young man, like most young people I tried to find my identity. The question, "Who am I?" was always on my mind. I was part of a family. Yet I was also an individual wasn't I? Was my identity merely wrapped up in my family? Or, was there more to me?

Like many people, I had siblings, but unlike most, I was a twin. As a twin, it was even harder to find my own distinctiveness. It seemed my very essence was tied to my twin brother. Mom thought it was cute to dress us in matching outfits—I hated it. Rarely did mom or dad call me by name. It was always, "You twins get cleaned up," or "Where have you twins been?" It was even worse in public. My brother and I looked so much alike that people were hopelessly confused. Whenever I ran an errand for mom or dad, I was greeted with, "Now, which one are you?" Teachers got us mixed up at school; relatives got us mixed up at reunions; and ministers got us mixed at synagogue. You can imagine why I was questioning whether or not birth predetermines a person's destiny.

I was a Jew born at the beginning of the first century. Rome ruled the world and occupied all of what used to be Israel. I lived in a small fishing town near the Sea of Galilee. Although not a fisherman himself, dad owned a small business and sold fish oil. The business was passed down from grandfather, and it was expected that my brother and I would continue in the trade. Did my culture—where I lived, or my father's occupation influence who I was and what I would become? Did I have any say in it or was it beyond my control?

As you might have guessed by now, I did a lot of thinking. In fact, it earned me a nickname: "Thinking Thomas." Some called me an intellectual. I liked to think of myself as pragmatic—practical, reasonable, or sensible. I liked to think things through, weigh the evidence, and try to determine the outcome. Because of this, other questions haunted me. Besides the "Who am I" question, I often wondered "Why am I here?" and "Does my life matter?" If I was never born would anyone have noticed or cared? What was life all about? I wanted to know life's purpose. I wanted to know the truth about life.

Ultimately, my quest for truth was a search for a way out. A way out of a small town. A way out of a predetermined life. A way out of selling fish oil. And even though I didn't have the answers to my questions, I was confident that I knew how to get them. *Education!* Education was the answer. Hence, I sought out the most educated people—the rabbis. Rabbis (or teachers) were the philosophers of our day. These were the ones that held the advanced degrees in science, philosophy, and theology. I believed following a rabbi was the only way to escape a life of selling fish oil. Rabbis, like me, thought things through. When faced with a question or problem they analyzed every possibility and logically came to a conclusion. Whenever a rabbi came to our area I'd make it a point to go and listen. I wanted so much to follow a rabbi. To become like one of them. To be free to become who I wanted to be. I just needed to select the right one.

Eventually, I did find the right one and all my questions about life and its purpose were answered—dramatically even! But the answers didn't come overnight. They began with a journey that lasted years. In fact, after some time, I gave up and quit searching because no one knew definitively. There were guesses, suppositions, ideas, and theories, but no absolute answers. Then I found that one, special rabbi. Or, perhaps more accurately, he found me. But I'm getting ahead of myself.

I was fourteen years old the first time I heard a rabbi; and I was captivated. The logic, the thought, the conclusions. Needless to say, I was impressed. But as the years went by and I listened to one after another, I found a common theme—arrogance. Not to mention, their conclusions were based on false premises and their answers fell flat. Most loved the adoration of the crowds more than truth, and their desire for the praise of man led them to answer questions based simply on popular opinion. The few that didn't— the few who were honestly searching, as I was—didn't have any more answers than me. I became disheartened and quit going to hear them speak. By then, well into my twenties, I was resigned to the unenviable conclusion that I would sell fish oil the rest of my life.

One spring day I was packaging fish oil to take to Jerusalem when my twin brother asked me a question, "Thomas, are going to stop to hear that strange fellow some call a rabbi when you get down around the Jordan River?"

"No; you know I quit going to hear those self-absorbed philosophers with no answers long ago," I responded.

"They say this guy is different."

"How so?" I asked.

"Well for one, he's not from the big city. He comes from the hill country of Judah and has an uncommon sensibility about him. Kind of a strange fellow, long hair, dresses in camel fur, wears a big leather belt; eats locusts and honey. They call him John—*John the Baptizer*. He's known for baptizing his disciples."

"Baptizing? That is strange," I replied.

He continued, "Outspoken too. 'In your face' kind of guy. Very sure of himself. Doesn't seem to care what people think of him. Straight forward, honest, and to the point. Think about it, sounds like a guy you might find interesting."

"Thanks, I'll keep it in mind. Do you want to go with me?" I asked.

"I would, but I need to take an order in the other direction up to Capernaum. Promised dad I'd have it up there by Friday," he said.

"Okay, I'm leaving in the morning. I'm traveling with about fifteen others heading to Jerusalem," I told him. Few people dared to travel alone in my day. Even with the protection Rome offered, there were too many bandits and other no-accounts lurking in the shadows to pounce on an unsuspecting lone traveler.

Four days later, our small band of travelers was walking south, not far from the Jordan River. Just before turning west, onto the Jerusalem Road, we came across a large crowd gathered in Bethany, a small village on the west bank of the river. "It's John; John the Baptizer!" a woman traveling with us yelled unable to hide her enthusiasm. "Let's stop!" another shouted. Soon our little caravan veered off the road and mingled with the on-lookers. As we drew near, we heard a rumbling in the crowd. I found myself standing next to a couple of fishermen.

"Excuse me, sir, what's going on?" I asked the one next to me.

"John was preaching when he was interrupted by some high-up religious types from Jerusalem. Apparently, they were sent from the temple to find out about John's ministry." He pointed, "Look, they're pushing their way to the front to question John."

"Huh," I said.

"My name's Andrew; what's yours?" he asked with a friendly smile.

"Thomas. Why are the temple authorities so concerned?"

"There's been some rumors floating about that John is the Christ," Andrew said.

"The Christ? The promised Messiah? You're kidding, right?"

Andrew didn't answer, he just shrugged his shoulders. The men had pushed themselves to the front and began to question John. It was clear to all that these temple officials were impressed with themselves. Arrogant, loud, and sarcastic, they put John on trial before the crowd demanding he identify himself. "Who are you?" one of them demanded.

John, like my brother said, didn't mix words. He went straight to the point, "I am not the Christ."

His accusers sneered. Trying their best to belittle him, they pressed him with a series of questions. The interrogation went back and forth.

"What then? Are you Elijah?"

"I am not."

"Are you the Prophet?"

"No."

And this is the testimony of John, when the Jews sent priests and Levites from Jerusalem to ask him, "Who are you?" He confessed, and did not deny, but confessed, "I am not the Christ." And they asked him, "What then? Are you Elijah?" He said, "I am not." "Are you the Prophet?" And he answered, "No." (John 1:19-21)

I was beginning to like John. He was frank and his answers

short. John still had the crowd on his side. Getting nowhere, his accusers became impatient and even more irritated. They continued demanding answers. Their questions hit close to home for someone like me.

"Who are you? We need to give an answer to those who sent us. What do you say about yourself?"

Those were the same questions I asked about myself. "Who am I?" "What do I have to say about myself?" Intrigued, I wondered what John's answer would be? Did he know who he was? Did he have the answers I was searching for?

John paused, and gazed steadily into the eyes of each of his adversaries. Then he turned his attention to the crowd and with a loud voice proclaimed, "I am the voice of one crying out in the wilderness, 'Make straight the way of the Lord'" Wow! What authority John spoke with! There's no question about what John believed. John knew who he was and what he was called to do. And he did it no matter what others thought.

> So they said to him, "Who are you? We need to give an answer to those who sent us. What do you say about yourself?" He said, "I am the voice of one crying out in the wilderness, 'Make straight the way of the Lord,' as the prophet Isaiah said." (John 1:22-23)

It became clear to me that these temple representatives weren't there to find the truth. They were there to trap John. They were trying to get him to claim to be some great prophet, or even the Christ. When this failed they turned to another line of questioning, "Then why are you baptizing, if you are neither the Christ, nor Elijah, nor the Prophet?"

Although I didn't like their attitude, it was a legitimate question. Why was John baptizing his followers? Baptism is a sign of new life. Baptism symbolized cleansing, removing guilt, making a new start.[1] John didn't answer like I expected. Rather than answering who he was, John pointed to another, "I baptize with water, but among you stands one you do not know, even he who comes after me, the strap of whose sandal I am not worthy to untie.'" It seems John's identity was tied to someone else.

> They asked him, "Then why are you baptizing, if you are neither the Christ, nor Elijah, nor the Prophet?" John answered them, "I baptize with water, but among you stands one you do not know, even he who comes after me, the strap of whose sandal I am not worthy to untie." These things took place in Bethany across the Jordan, where John was baptizing. (John 1:25-28)

With that John was done. He didn't care to answer any more questions, and he didn't. He just turned and walked away. Some in the crowd, including Andrew and the other fisherman, followed John. Most, like me, returned to our business.

The last leg of the journey to Jerusalem was filled with talk about John. It was clear the religious leaders in Jerusalem didn't like John, and his popularity with the common people angered them.

Being more of a thinker than a talker, I listened, and kept to myself. John's self-assurance impressed me. He had what I longed for; a sense of identity—and purpose. He knew who he was and why he was here and dove headlong into life. What a way to live! He had a sense of purpose and calling. Yes, that was it. He was called by something—or *someone*—greater than himself to fulfill a purpose greater than his own life. John's words puzzled me. His identity was wrapped in someone greater than himself. Someone who gave his life direction and purpose. Someone he said, *"You do not know."*

Who is this one who stands among us that we do not know? John said that he comes after him; and that John was not worthy to untie his sandals. Hence, he is greater than John.

～

After completing my business in Jerusalem, I headed home. On the way back, we stopped to take a break at the spot where the religious leaders challenged John. In less than a week the crowds were gone. John himself seemed to have disappeared from the scene. No doubt he was a politically charged figure and rumor had it Herod was looking to arrest him. I also wondered where the fishermen, Andrew and his friend, had gone.

When I got home, I told my brother about the encounter with John the Baptizer and how he was everything my brother said he was. "Unlike the other rabbis, John is authentic and certain of himself and his message," I said.

"What's his message?"

"He was preaching a baptism of repentance for the forgiveness of sins."

"Now that's interesting. Forgiveness of sins. I suppose we all need our sins forgiven," my brother mused.

"Yes, but he also said there's one coming after him. One greater than he," I said.

"I wonder if he's talking about the man called Jesus."

"Who is Jesus?" I asked.

"Haven't you heard? Oh, that's right you've been out of town. Jesus has been teaching all around the area the past couple of days. Some say he's even healing people. Sounds like he's preaching the same message you say John was, "Repent, the kingdom of God is at hand." He's speaking this afternoon down by the old swimming hole where the fishermen pull their boats ashore. I plan on going. Why don't you come with me?"

That afternoon my brother and I gathered with a large crowd. Jesus was obviously making an impression. He had quickly amassed a large following of disciples. People assembled on the slope of a hill that leveled out as it reached the rocky shore where three fishing boats sat beached. The people in front started to take a seat on the grass and I saw four men push one of the boats into the water. A fifth man was standing in the boat. They anchored the boat thirty feet from the shore.

My brother and I worked our way closer and sat with the crowd. I surmised that Jesus was the one standing in the boat. Then I recognized Andrew and his friend as two of the four men who helped anchor the boat. The other two helpers were also fishermen I recognized from the area, John and James, I believed were their names. I thought Andrew was one of John's disciples, but here he was with Jesus.

Standing in the boat, Jesus raised his hands and a hush fell on the crowd. He began to speak, "The time is fulfilled, and the kingdom of God is at hand; repent and believe the gospel."[2] Jesus preached for over an hour, and I was captivated. He, like John, spoke with authority. He quoted scripture and explained hard to understand passages—clearly and simply. He preached the forgiveness of sins apart from the works of the law, which was something I never heard before. But the way he explained it made perfect sense. More than anything he preached that God's kingdom was here. I wanted to hear more. I planned to attend synagogue on Saturday; Jesus was the scheduled guest teacher.

Jesus' synagogue message did it for me. This man had the answers. He taught *as one who had authority, and not as the scribes* who simply read from the Hebrew text. Jesus spent some weeks in and around Galilee and I was there each time he spoke. After preaching, Jesus often sought solitude to pray for an hour or so. One evening he did just that, as was his custom, he ascended a mountain to pray.

Several of us waited for his return, but after some time, we all fell asleep. In the morning twelve of us received the surprise of our lives. We were chosen to be apostles—messengers for him. We would speak for him!

In these days he went out to the mountain to pray, and all night he continued in prayer to God. And when day came, he called his disciples and chose from them twelve, whom he named apostles: Simon, whom he named Peter, and Andrew his brother, and James and John, and Philip, and Bartholomew, and Matthew, and Thomas, and James the son of Alphaeus, and Simon who was called the Zealot, and Judas the son of James, and Judas Iscariot, who became a traitor. (Luke 6:12-16)

Being named among the Twelve was a great privilege and a great responsibility. As you already know, I wasn't much of a talker, but more of a thinker. In fact, there are only four short statements recorded of me speaking in the Gospels. I'd like to highlight each one. The first reveals my doubt about Jesus' judgment.

The first few months with Jesus flew by. He had power from God to heal the sick and he gave some of that power to us. We too were able to heal, cast out demons, and preach the coming of God's kingdom with authority. But, just like John, the temple rulers became suspicious and envious of Jesus. I guess they didn't like the crowds following Jesus, not to mention Jesus embarrassing them time and again.

I recall one occasion in Jerusalem where Jesus narrowly

escaped being stoned to death. Jesus' message didn't fit too well with the religious leaders. They even accused Jesus of blasphemy, a crime punishable by death under Jewish law. They were about to start throwing rocks when Jesus asked them, "I have shown you many good works from the Father; for which of them are you going to stone me?"

"How ridiculous was that charge?" I thought.

Jesus responded, again quoting scripture, but they weren't happy and tried to arrest him.

The Jews picked up stones again to stone him. Jesus answered them, "I have shown you many good works from the Father; for which of them are you going to stone me?" The Jews answered him, "It is not for a good work that we are going to stone you but for blasphemy, because you, being a man, make yourself God." (John 10:31-33)

"It is not for a good work that we are going to stone you but for blasphemy, because you, being a man, make yourself God." Again they sought to arrest him, but he escaped from their hands. He went away again across the Jordan to the place where John had been baptizing at first, and there he remained. And many came to him. And they said, "John did no sign, but everything that John said about this man was true." And many believed in him there. (John 10:39-42)

We left Jerusalem and stopped at the Jordan River where I first heard John preach. It was there, at the Jordan River, we heard the tragic news of Lazarus' sudden and unexpected death. Lazarus, not one of the Twelve, but a good friend of Jesus, lived with his two sisters just outside Jerusalem in a town called Bethany (Not to be confused with the Bethany located west of the Jordan River, where

I first heard John the Baptizer preach.). The report that Lazarus was ill came two days before Jesus announced his death. At first, we didn't understand, and thought that Lazarus was merely sick and would soon be up and around again when Jesus spelled it out plainly for us, "Lazarus has died."

Why? I wondered. Why should we go back to Jerusalem? Did Jesus forget they just tried to arrest and kill him? Besides, Lazarus would be buried by the time we got there. The funeral would be over, and Jesus will be of no help. Before I realized it, I was blurting out, "Let us also go, that we may die with him." There were escalating threats on Jesus' life and while I truly thought this maybe the end, I held out hope that it wasn't. As it turned out, no harm came to us.

Then Jesus told them plainly, "Lazarus has died, and for your sake I am glad that I was not there, so that you may believe. But let us go to him." So Thomas, called the Twin, said to his fellow disciples, "Let us also go, that we may die with him." (John 11:14-16)

You may know the story. We went to Bethany and Jesus raised Lazarus from the dead. This was the third person he raised from the dead, but Lazarus was different from the other two, the widow's son and Jairus' daughter. Both of them were younger and had just died. Some falsely reported that they were only sick and Jesus healed them. But there was no question with Lazarus, he was dead as dead could be and nobody could deny it. His body was in the tomb four days. In fact, his sister, Martha, objected to opening the tomb because of the odor. Nevertheless, Jesus raised Lazarus to life.

My next words recorded in scripture reveal how desperate I was to hold onto the security I felt when I was in Jesus' presence. I finally had a sense of purpose and direction. Gone was the sense of misdirection that had overwhelmed me. After all, if we don't know where we are going, how can we know the way to get there?

We were eating the Passover meal. Although we didn't know it at the time, it was Jesus' last meal before his death. It's the meal that famously came to be known as the "Last Supper." Not realizing Jesus' death was pending, it was a joyous occasion for me and the other apostles. We were laughing and making small talk when Jesus began talking about going away by himself and we apostles following him after some time. Peter objected and as was his manner, bluntly asked, "Lord, where are you going?"

We all thought Jesus was preparing to set up his throne in Jerusalem and we planned on ruling with him. Some months back, we recognized Jesus as the Christ—the promised Messiah and one promised to sit on David's throne in Jerusalem. Now he was talking about leaving us. That wasn't what we'd planned.

Jesus responded to Peter, "Where I am going you cannot follow me now, but you will follow afterward."

> Little children, yet a little while I am with you. You will seek me, and just as I said to the Jews, so now I also say to you, 'Where I am going you cannot come.'...Simon Peter said to him, "Lord, where are you going?" Jesus answered him, "Where I am going you cannot follow me now, but you will follow afterward." (John 13:33, 36)

Jesus continued explaining that he would be preparing a place for us to live so he could return and get us. "I will come again and will take you to myself, that where I am you may be also. And you know the way to where I am going."

Wait. Where was he going that we couldn't go with him? Everywhere he went, we were with him—right at his side through thick and thin. If we didn't know where he was going, how were we to know the way? I asked him, "Lord, we do not know where you are going. How can we know the way?'"

His response to me is now one of the most concise and doctrine filled statements about salvation Jesus made. This is what Jesus said, "I am the way, and the truth, and the life. No one comes to the Father except through me."

And if I go and prepare a place for you, I will come again and will take you to myself, that where I am you may be also. And you know the way to where I am going." Thomas said to him, "Lord, we do not know where you are going. How can we know the way?" Jesus said to him, "I am the way, and the truth, and the life. No one comes to the Father except through me. (John 14:3-6)

Jesus, himself, is the way? The way where? "To the Father," he said. God the Father is in heaven. Jesus is going to heaven and then coming back to get us? That seemed to be what he said, but it didn't make any sense. Maybe I just misunderstood, or didn't have all the facts. I'd have to think on that a while.

Little did I know, I wouldn't have much time to think about what Jesus said. Only a few short hours later saw us in the garden when one of our own, Judas Iscariot, brought a contingent of Jewish religious leaders and temple guards to arrest Jesus. He was hauled in before a Jewish court facing trumped-up charges of blasphemy.

After following Jesus for nearly three years, everything came to a sudden and unexpected end. The trial before the Jewish court was a sham. No evidence. No witnesses. Nothing. Nothing—until Jesus claimed to be God himself to the council. The chief priest flew into a rage and condemned Jesus to death for his assertion. I, too, was stunned by Jesus' pronouncement. What did Jesus mean that he was God? We apostles acknowledged he was the Son of God, just as King David, and all the other kings were "sons of God" in the political sense. And the prophet Ezekiel used the term son of man, as did Jesus. But neither the kings nor the prophets ever claimed to *be* God.

Had I misread Jesus? For three years I followed him. For three years I listened to his teaching. His life was authentic. He lived what he preached. He was gifted and performed miracles, healing the sick and raising the dead. Who was he? I thought he was the Messiah. But why would his own people reject him? Why would a king of Israel claim to be God?

I left the trial with my head down and walked out into the streets of Jerusalem. The sun was just coming up and the Jewish authorities planned to take Jesus before the Roman court presided over by Pilate. They were bent on having Jesus put to death but didn't have the authority to do so. Pilate did. Pilate was a spineless weasel who'd do anything for political gain. He put his own position above justice and bent to the will of the mob. Jesus wouldn't have a chance.

I was right. That very day, Jesus was crucified just hours after making the outrageous claim of being God. I wasn't there to witness his horrific beating and death, but I did walk out to the site and see where he was hanged and flanked by Roman guards. John was there. I kept my distance. Disappointed, I walked away. What now? Jesus was dead, betrayed by one of his own. Judas, who I had considered a friend, hanged himself after betraying Jesus. But, what will happen to the rest of us? Will the authorities arrest us? For the next three days, I drifted around Jerusalem hiding from the authorities and thinking about how everything I hoped for was gone.

My thoughts went to home. Dad had turned the business over to my brother. He and his boys were running it and doing well. What would I do? Those haunting questions came rushing back, "Who am I?" "Why am I here?" "Does my life matter?" I thought Jesus was the answer and now he is dead.

Being pragmatic, I knew I needed to do something and I knew fish oil. So, I decided to return home. But before leaving Jerusalem, I'd try to drum up some business. The Monday after Jesus' death, I was up early and heading for the market when I heard someone calling my name, "Thomas! Thomas!" The familiar voice was John's. I turned around to see John and James running toward me. I thought they seem rather chipper considering they only recently buried a friend and their dreams all in one day.

"Yes, what is it?" I asked curtly not really wanting to talk.

"We have seen the Lord," they responded.

"What? Are you kidding me?" I thought, Yea, I saw him too, hanging dead on a Roman cross. For four days I'd been racked by depression, doubt, and fear, all because of false hope. I gave them a piece of my mind, "Unless I see in his hands the mark of the nails, and place my finger into the mark of the nails, and place my hand into his side, I will never believe." With that I turned on my heels and walked away. The gall of them! They have seen Jesus. Hogwash.

Now Thomas, one of the twelve, called the Twin, was not with them when Jesus came. So the other disciples told him, "We have seen the Lord." But he said to them, "Unless I see in his hands the mark of the nails, and place my finger into the mark of the nails, and place my hand into his side, I will never believe." (John 20:24-25)

"Come to Mark's house on Sunday. We'll all be there," John shouted as I stormed away.

I stayed in and near the market for the next few days. I made a lot of new contacts and even took some orders. I planned on leaving for home as soon as possible, but business continued to keep me stuck in Jerusalem. The way things were going it looked like I'd have to stay at least a week. I consoled myself that at least I was safe from running into any of the other apostles by sticking close to the stalls of merchants.

But, try as I may, I couldn't shake John's invitation. Reluctantly, I went to Mark's house. It was now over a week since Jesus' death. I really didn't want to deal with the others, but half of them were fishermen. Maybe I could make some deals. When I got to the house, I was surprised to find everyone in a good mood. Mark's mother welcomed me and gave me a big hug. "Isn't it great!" she said, locking the door securely behind me.

"What's that?" I asked.

Clearly puzzled, she looked up at me, "Jesus. Why, Jesus is risen! Haven't you heard?"

"Oh, yea, John said something about that," I said handing her my cloak. Pragmatic people can be rather joyless at times; and I was as pragmatic as they came. I think she sensed my disparaging spirit and said no more about Jesus.

"There's stew on the stove, help yourself," she said with a timid smile exchanging my cloak for a bowl and spoon.

"Thank you," I said, heading for the stove. I scooped a healthy portion of the inviting stew into my bowl.

"Thomas is here," Bartholomew announced when I appeared at the entrance to the large living room.

Tentatively, I walked into the room holding the bowl with both hands to avoid hugs and kisses. "I'm here on business," I thought to myself forcing a smile and nodding my head acknowledging my friends. The room was dim, but the candle light revealed the faces of the other apostles. All ten were present.

Suddenly, a burst of light illuminated the room! It was nearly blinding. Then it was gone. I blinked. "What was that?" I wondered. Then I saw Jesus standing before me. He announced to the room, "Peace be with you."

Jesus then turned to face me and compassionately said, "Put your finger here, and see my hands; and put out your hand, and place it in my side. Do not disbelieve, but believe."

The bowl of stew dropped from my hands and I fell to my knees. He is God! I looked up to Jesus and proclaimed, "My Lord and my God!"

Looking down, his eyes still filled with love, he said, "Have you believed because you have seen me? Blessed are those who have not seen and yet have believed."

Eight days later, his disciples were inside again, and Thomas was with them. Although the doors were locked, Jesus came and stood among them and said, "Peace be with you." Then he said to Thomas, "Put your finger here, and see my hands; and put out your hand, and place it in my side. Do not disbelieve, but believe." Thomas answered him, "My Lord and my God!" Jesus said to him, "Have you believed because you have seen me? Blessed are those who have not seen and yet have believed." (John 20:26-29)

～

I t took Thomas seeing the resurrected Christ to believe. Jesus responded to Thomas' declaration that he is God, "Blessed are those who have not seen and yet have believed."

Easter is the celebration of the risen Christ. Jesus came the first time to die for us and providing forgiveness for our sins by his death, burial, and resurrection. Jesus told Thomas, "I am the way, and the truth, and the life. No one comes to the Father except through me" (John 14:6). Do you believe? Have you put your faith in Jesus alone for salvation?

REFERENCES

Blue Letter Bible. (n.d.). Retrieved May 27, 2011, from http://www.blueletterbible.org/index.cfm

Brisco, T. V. (1998). *Holman Bible Atlas.* Nashville: Broadman and Holman Publishers.

Carson, D. (1991). *Pillar New Testament Commentary, John.* Grand Rapids: Wm. B. Eerdmans Publishing Company.

Furguson, S. B. (1988). *The Sermon on the Mount.* Edinburgh: Banner of Truth.

Grudem, W. (1994). *Systematic Theology.* Grand Rapids, MI, USA: Zondervan.

Henry, M. (1991). *Matthew Henry's Commentary on the Whole Bible.* Peabody: Hendrickson Publishers.

Holman. (1992). *Holman Bible Handbook.* Nashville: Holman Bible Publishers.

Kruse, C. G. (2003). *Tyndale New Testament Commentaries, John.* Downers Grove: Inter-Varsity Press.

Moo, D. J. (1996). *The Espistle to the Romans, The New International Commentary on the New Testament.* (G. D. Fee, Ed.) Grand Rapids, MI, USA: Wm. B. Eerdmans Publishing Comp.

Morris, L. (1998). *Tyndale NT Commentaries, Luke* (Vol. 3). Dowers Grove: InterVarsity Press.

Mounce, R. H. (1997). *The New International Commentary of the New Testament, Revelation.* Grand Rapids: Eerdmans.

Nelson's New Illustrated Bible Dictionary. (1995). *Nelson's New Illustrated Bible Dictionary.* (R. F. Youngblood, Ed.) Nashville, TN, USA: Thomas Nelson Pulishers.

Osborne, G. (2004). *Romans, the IVP New Testament Commentary Series* (Vol. 6). (G. Osborne, Ed.) Madison, WI, USA: InterVarsity Press.

Osborne, G. R. (2002). *Baker Exegetical Commentary on the New Testament, Revelation.* Grand Rapids: Baker Academic.

Ross, A. (2017). *The Priests.* Retrieved from Bible.org: bible.org/seriespage/priests#P7_296

Stuart, D. K. (2006). *The New American Commentary, Exodus, Vol. 2.* B&H Publishing Group: Nashville.

The Editors of Encyclopædia Britannica. (2015). *Hazael, King of Damascus.* Retrieved from Encyclopedia Britannnica: http://www.britannica.com/biography/Hazael

Unger, M. (1988). *The New Ungers Bible Dictionary.* Chicago: Moody Press.

Unger, M. (2005). *The New Unger's Bible Handbook.* Chicago: Moody Press.

Vine, W. U. (1996). Vine's Complete Expository Dictionary of Old and New Testament Words. Nashville: Thomas Nelson Publishers.

WebMD. (2005-2017). *WebMD.* Retrieved from WebMD: webmd.com/skin-problems-and-treatments/guide/leprosy-symptoms-treatments-history

Whiston, W. (1992). *The Works of Flavius Josephus* (Vols. I-IV). Grand Rapids: Baker Book House Company.

Zondervan. (1999). *Zondervan Handbook to the Bible.* Grand Rapids: Zondervan.

NOTES

1. A Warrior with a Problem

1. (Youngblood, 1995, p. 171)
2. (Blue Letter Bible)
3. (Source: webmd.com/skin-problems-and-treatments/guide/leprosy-symptoms-treatments-history; Accessed June 25, 2014)

2. The Lord Remembers

1. (Ross, Allan retrieved from: bible.org/seriespage/priests#P7_296; September 23, 2014)
2. (Historians place the birth of Christ anywhere from 4-6 BC)
3. (Blue Letter Bible)
4. (Morris, 1998, p. 85)
5. See Gen. 17:12; and Lev. 12:3

5. Bitter to the End

1. (See Josephus, *Ant. 7.1.3*)
2. (Psalm 23)

6. Almost Persuaded

1. (Acts 8:26b)
2. (Acts 12:23)
3. (Unger, 1988, pp. 563-564)
4. (Youngblood, 1995, p. 562)

8. The Inn Crowd

1. (Bock, 2003, pp. 202-203)

9. Pragmatic Belief

1. (Dockery, 2001, p. 4)
2. (Mark 1:15)

ABOUT THE AUTHOR

 Tim Rupp was a career police officer before being called into full-time vocational ministry. He enlisted in the Air Force after graduating high school. After his enlistment, Tim joined the San Antonio Police Department (SAPD) and gave 24 years of dedicated service before retiring in 2007. During his SAPD career he worked as a patrol officer, homicide detective, patrol sergeant, sex crimes sergeant, police academy supervisor, and internal affairs sergeant-investigator. He continued his law enforcement service as a reserve deputy with the Bonneville County Sheriff's Office, Idaho from 2009-2020.

Before retiring from the SAPD, Tim was called to pastor Elm Creek Baptist Church in La Vernia, TX, just outside of San Antonio. Following his retirement in 2007, he was called to pastor full-time in Idaho Falls, where he pastored until 2020. In 2016, Tim founded The Strong Blue Line Ministries to law enforcement officers. In 2017, he and a group active and retired police officers planted Cop Church Idaho Falls. In 2020, Tim retired from being a full-time pastor to cofound the Law Enforcement Chaplaincy of Idaho and committed to serving LEOs and their families full-time. He is available to teach seminars for police officers, churches, and men's groups. For more information or to contact Tim, go to TheStrongBlueLine.org.

Tim graduated from Texas State University (Master of Science in Criminal Justice), Southwestern Baptist Theological Seminary (Master of Divinity and Master of Arts in Christian Education), and Western Seminary (Doctor of Ministry). He is married to Sherry and they have three children, Christina, Aaron, and Emily and several grandchildren.

OTHER TITLES BY TIM RUPP

Available on Amazon or in bulk order at The Strong Blue Line (TheStrongBlueLine.org).

Non-Fiction:

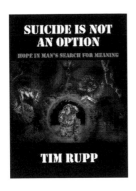

Suicide is Not an Option, Hope in Man's Search for Meaning, 2020.

America's law enforcement officers are significantly more likely to die by suicide than being murdered in the line of duty. Mental health professionals have come alongside officers with treatment, assistance, and counsel. Yet, the suicide rate continues to increase. Can this ever-increasing suicide rate among these warriors be stopped? In *Suicide is Not an Option*, Rupp approaches suicide from a spiritual health perspective. His police experience enables him to relate the challenges faced by officers today. Using personal accounts, clear language, and practical reasoning, Rupp argues there is meaning to life beyond the individual. A meaning so deep it transcends life on earth. Humans are not only physical and mental beings, but spiritual beings who yearn for a yet to be experienced life beyond. This eternal hope instilled in every person gives meaning to life and a reason to hope. Hope for more, hope for new, hope for better. Intrinsic hope is a key to reduce not only the suicide rate among our warriors, but across humanity.

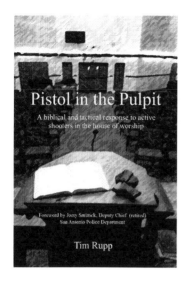

Pistol in the Pulpit, A biblical and tactical response to active shootings in the house of worship, 2016.

Active Shooter—a term recently coined that sends chills up the spines of principles, teachers, parents...and now pastors and parishioners. The FBI defines an active shooter as "an individual actively engaged in killing or attempting to kill people in a confined and populated area, typically through the use of firearms." Active Killer is a more fitting term. What is the biblical approach to this threat? Christians are struggling with how to respond. Do we trust God and pray for his protection? Do we "turn the other cheek" and do nothing when someone threatens to kill us? Do we take up arms to defend ourselves and others? Christians who choose the responsibility of employing lethal force must be informed by both a spiritual and tactical foundation. Not only is there a proper biblical response, there is also a proper tactical response. What are these proper responses? These critical questions are answered in *Pistol in the Pulpit*.

Winning a Gunfight, Securing victory ethically, mentally, and tactically in a gunfight, 2016.

Does physically surviving a gunfight mean you won? Not by a long shot. Many people survive gunfights. In fact, most people who are in a gunfight survive. But there's a difference between surviving and winning. Surviving means you continue to exist. Continuing to exist and winning are not the same.

Career police officer and author Tim Rupp has been on both sides of a gunfight—being investigated after being in a gunfight and investigating citizens and officers who have been in shootings. Drawing from personal and professional experiences, Rupp takes you through what you'll face in a gunfight. Before picking up a gun for personal protection or the protection of others you need to prepare yourself for what you'll face before, during, and after a gunfight. *Winning a Gunfight* prepares you ethically, mentally, and tactically how to win a gunfight. *Winning a Gunfight* is a must read for police officers, military, and armed citizens.

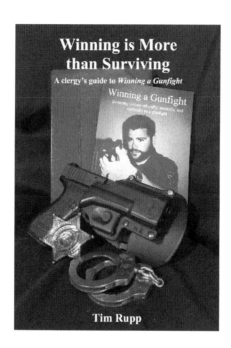

Winning is More than Surviving, A clergy's guide to *Winning a Gunfight, 2018.*

Police and military chaplains are called on to minister to those who kill.

Violence is shunned in our society, but justified violence is sometimes necessary to stop unjustified violence. Even the wise King Solomon said, there is "a time to kill" (Ecc. 3:3). While most of society recoils in fear at violence, some are called to enter that violent world and protect.

There are warriors among us who take up arms and protect those unable or unwilling to protect themselves. But who helps the warriors? Chaplains are called to minister to the spiritual needs of these warriors. To be effective, members of the clergy need to understand the dynamics of using lethal force. *Winning is More than Surviving* is a supplemental guide to *Winning a Gunfight* for clergy to use as they minister to these warriors.

A Preaching Primer, Basic Homiletics, 2021

Preaching is simple. It can be defined as, "Speaking God's word to people." However, preaching is also complex. It is both an art and a science. It is both a gift and a task. It will bring out the best or the worse in people.

In this primer, Pastor Tim Rupp walks the student-preacher step-by-step how to write and deliver a biblically based expository sermon.

Fiction:

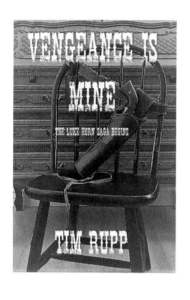

Vengeance Is Mine, The Luke Horn Saga Begins, 2017.

It was 1863, America was split by war. Texas farmer and former lawman, Levi Horn is called to serve for the South, leaving his teenage son to watch over the family. A band of outlaws led by a revenge-driven escaped convict attacks Horn's family and farm. Torn between vengeance and justice, sixteen-year-old Luke Horn sets off on the trail of the outlaws.

Vengeance Is Mine Too, The Luke Horn Saga Continues, 2019.

Just when you think the adventure is over, you find it just began. Luke, Joe Ray, and Jack aren't finished righting wrongs. The Civil War was tearing America apart and renegade Confederate soldiers were wreaking havoc in Texas. The outlaw soldiers made the mistake of thinking Luke was still a boy. He wasn't. Luke was forced into

manhood and accepted the responsibilities manhood demands while he struggled with his own demons.

Vengeance Is His, The Luke Horn Saga Book III, 2021.

"I bounded to my feet, spun, pointed the .44 at the man with pistol. His gun was still pointed at my bedroll I pressed my index finger, the pistol recoiled in my hand. Trusting that my shot hit its mark, I thumbed the hammer back and turned to face the other two..."

Luke didn't start it, but he was ready to finish it.

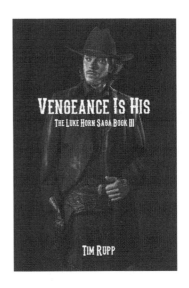

Made in the USA
Columbia, SC
25 July 2024

39296632R00104